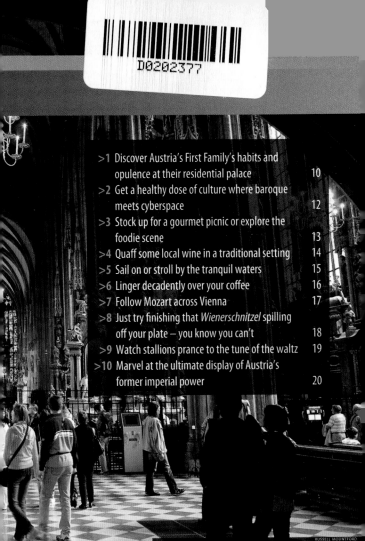

D0202377

RUSSELL MOUNTFORD

Walk beneath the soaring arched ceiling of Stephansdom (p46)

V

HIGHLIGHTS

>1 SCHLOSS SCHÖNBRUNN

DISCOVER AUSTRIA'S FIRST FAMILY'S HABITS AND OPULENCE AT THEIR RESIDENTIAL PALACE

With its grandiose proportions, you'd never guess this baroque palace is in fact the downsized version of the structure originally planned for this site.

The name Schloss Schönbrunn comes from the Schöner Brunnen (beautiful fountain) that was built around a spring discovered when Emperor Matthias (1557–1619) went out hunting and struck water instead. A pleasure palace was built at the site by Ferdinand II in 1637, only to be razed by the Turks in 1683. Soon after, Leopold I commissioned Johann Bernhard Fischer von Erlach to build a luxurious summer palace. Fischer von Erlach came up with hugely ambitious plans for one that would dwarf Versailles and be situated on the hill where the Gloriette now stands. The plans were deemed too expensive and a less elaborate construction was completed in 1700.

Maria Theresia, upon her accession to the throne in 1740, chose Schönbrunn as the seat for her family and her court. The young architect Nikolaus Pacassi was commissioned to renovate and extend the palace,

and work was carried out from 1744 to 1749. The interior was fitted out in rococo style and, upon completion of the renovations, the palace had some 2000 rooms, as well as a chapel and a theatre. Like most imperial buildings associated with Maria Theresia, the exterior was painted her favourite colour, which has come to be known as *Schönbrunngelb* (Schönbrunn yellow).

The Habsburgs were not the palace's only famous residents, as Napoleon took it over from 1805 to 1809. Karl I turned out the lights for the Habsburgs when he abdicated in the Blue Chinese Salon in 1918; the palace became the property of the new republic. Bomb damage was suffered during WWII, restoration of which was completed in 1955.

Tours of Schloss Schönbrunn focus on its illustrious residents. This means you get to see majestic spaces and hear the background stories about what Austria's famous family did where. The Round Chinese Room displays a hidden doorway where Maria Theresia held her secret consultations, and the Napoleon Room contains the crested lark favoured by his son. But both are overshadowed by the Millions Room's Persian miniatures set on rosewood panels; the room is named after the sum Maria Theresia paid for the decorations. See p117 for our full review of Schloss Schönbrunn.

RICHARD NEBESKY

>2 MUSEUMSQUARTIER

GET A HEALTHY DOSE OF CULTURE WHERE BAROQUE MEETS CYBERSPACE

The MuseumsQuartier (MQ) makes the heady claim of being among the world's 10 largest cultural complexes. With roughly 60,000 sq metres of exhibition space housed in baroque and modern structures, we believe them. Heavyweights such as the Leopold Museum (p59), filled with 19th- and 20th-century art; Museum Moderner Kunst (MUMOK; p59), Austria's largest modern-art museum; and temporary exhibition hall Kunsthalle (p58) all reside here among stylish cafes and restaurants.

Despite the obvious hype, this cultural district is absolutely idiosyn- cratic and unique. It has succeeded in the tough act of bringing together heritage and the avante-garde. The historic part consists of former sta- bles dating from 1725, designed by Johann Bernhard Fischer von Erlach. The *Haupthof* (main plaza; pictured below) is used for events and hosts both winter and summer programs. It's especially popular during the summer months – everyone gets to work on their tans while lounging on postmodern seating (each year, the seats are painted a different colour).

KRZYSZTOF DYDYNSKI

>3 NASCHMARKT

STOCK UP FOR A GOURMET PICNIC OR EXPLORE THE FOODIE SCENE

The Naschmarkt (p86) puts all other markets to shame. This massive strip of stalls and restaurants extends for more than 500m along Linke Wienzeile between Kettenbrückengasse and Karlsplatz. The western end, near Kettenbrückengasse, is more fun, with all sorts of meats, fruit and vegetables (this is *the* place for that hard-to-find exotic variety), spices, wines, cheeses and olives, Indian and Middle Eastern specialities, and fabulous kebab and falafel stands. The market peters out at the eastern end to stalls selling Indian fabrics, jewellery and trashy trinkets – you may suddenly feel like you're in a Nepali tourist town.

Wedged between the stalls and snack joints are some of Vienna's trendiest restaurants, many with floor-to-ceiling glass walls. Dine in one and you'll feel distinctly like you're inside a fishbowl. But when the sun shines, the dining action spills out of the bowl and you'll find shades-toting Viennese fighting for a spot at the outdoor tables. All this action turns the Naschmarkt into a festive cacophony of fun, so don't be surprised if hours go by and you find you're still here.

GREG ELMS

13

V

HIGHLIGHTS

>4 HEURIGEN

QUAFF SOME LOCAL WINE IN A TRADITIONAL SETTING

Vienna is the only world capital that produces significant quantities of wine within its city limits. No surprise, then, that *Heurigen* (wine taverns; pictured below, Mayer am Pfarrplatz, p80) define Vienna's cultural and culinary scene. These simple establishments date back to the Middle Ages, but it was Joseph II who first officially granted producers the right to sell their wine from their own premises, in 1784.

Heurigen are rustic, with basic wooden tables and a large garden or inner courtyard. Food is served buffet-style; blood sausage, pickled vegetables, potato salad and strudel are the mainstays. Tart wine, traditionally made by the owner and usually only a year old, is best mixed with soda water. *Sturm* (literally 'storm', for its cloudy appearance and chaotic effects) is fermented grape juice with high alcohol content and a deceptively sweet, nonlethal taste. It's available around September to mid-October.

Stadtheurigen reside in the city's urban confluence and are often very basic affairs with tiny inner courtyards or multileveled cellars.

Heurigen are concentrated in and around Vienna's suburbs. Many are only open part of the year, or every other month. Luckily, if one is closed, one next door is often open. Just look for the *Heuriger* ID: a *Busch'n* (green wreath or branch) hanging over its door.

KRZYSZTOF DYDYNSKI

>5 THE THREE BLUE DANUBES
SAIL ON OR STROLL BY THE TRANQUIL WATERS

Appreciating the illustrious Danube is all about getting out there. Few rivers define a country and its most romantic tune like the Danube does. Sail its waters or stroll, cycle or simply relax on its shores for a whopping dose of nature.

Cycling around here is easy, and a great way to discover how the three Danubes coexist in the capital. The first, the Danube Canal, cuts between the city centre and Leopoldstadt, the district immediately to its east. The second, the Neue Donau (New Danube), is a new channel born when the Donauinsel (an artificial island) was created in the 1970s. Further east lies the Alte Donau (Old Danube), a dead end of a former branch of the Danube, separated from the Neue Donau by a dam. Since the Alte Donau no longer has any direct connection to the river, it's actually a crescent-shaped lake. One thing all the waterways boast is tranquillity. They ripple to their own slow waltz, in typical Viennese fashion, and eschew all that is hurried.

Its shores can be another story, however. The Donauinsel (p113) hops to a hip beat in the summer, when a constellation of bars lines its shores. Squint a little and you'd think you're in the Med.

RICHARD NEBESKY

>6 KAFFEEHÄUSER

LINGER DECADENTLY OVER YOUR COFFEE

The Viennese are obsessed with their coffee rituals and coffee houses, which are places to halt a busy schedule and replenish the system.

Coffee houses graced Vienna's alleyways for centuries. Legend has it that coffee beans were left behind by the fleeing Turks in 1683, and by 1685 the first house had opened in the first district. Their popularity grew, and by the 19th century there were a reputed 600 in business.

Traditional coffee houses, such as Café Sperl (pictured below; p66), come in a number of guises: the grand affairs of the 19th-century share the streets with *Jugendstil* (art nouveau) delights and post-WWII establishments. *Konditoreien* (cake shops), with seating and invariably an older clientele, are also commonplace.

No matter the decor, the environment is the same – paused. Nothing moves fast. Patrons devour newspapers and magazines at their leisure, and pressure to order a second cup is nonexistent. Waiters command their own genus: arrogant and scolding one minute, courteous the next. They are charming in their peculiar way of going about their business.

Coffee is king, but most coffee houses offer a full food and drink menu, making them excellent options for anything from a bite to a meal with an alcoholic beverage.

RICHARD NEBESKY

>7 MOZART

FOLLOW MOZART ACROSS VIENNA

Like Haydn, Schubert and Beethoven, Wolfgang Amadeus Mozart came to Vienna in search of the Habsburgs' ready money, and he remained here until his death. His tenure in Vienna (1780–91) marks the period when he produced some of his greatest pieces, and the world's best classical music.

It's no surprise, then, that there are a slew of sights dedicated to the master, and Mozart look-alikes peddle tickets to concerts at busy tourist spots throughout the city. From the Mozart statue at the Burggarten (p38) to the Mozarthaus (p42), where the great composer lived and penned some of his work, you'll find him everywhere. You can also catch a Mozart concert in a space where he once rehearsed, at Schönbrunn's Orangery (pictured below; p123).

The pieces he wrote here – among them *The Marriage of Figaro* (1786), *Don Giovanni* (1787), *Così fan Tutte* (1790) and *The Magic Flute* (1791) – represent some of the best elements of Mozart: drama, comedy, intimacy and a whole heap of ingenuity. The Staatsoper (p55), where he opened *Don Giovanni*, frequently stages this and other works by the master, such as *The Magic Flute*.

Mozart was buried in an unmarked grave in St Marxer Friedhof (p101), in line with funeral rites at that time as decreed by Emperor Joseph II, which stated: 'The sole purpose of burial is the rapid decomposition of the body.' Despite countless attempts, the exact location of his grave has never been determined.

KRZYSZTOF DYDYNSKI

>8 BEISLN

JUST TRY FINISHING THAT *WIENERSCHNITZEL* SPILLING OFF YOUR PLATE – YOU KNOW YOU CAN'T

This species of restaurant is unique to Vienna. You can spot an original by a number of key attributes. One, it's a beer house featuring wood panelling and plain tables. Two, there's likely a ceramic oven wedged in a corner. Three, hearty Viennese cuisine dominates. This is where you want to eat a schnitzel, followed by a serving of *Kaiserschmarrn* (sweetened pancakes with raisins) for dessert. By and large, they are inexpensive options and attract a loyal following of locals.

Recently, marginally more expensive *neo-Beisln* have emerged. These eateries shake things up a bit: some add new touches to old recipes; others break tradition with modern furnishings or – gasp – contain a trendy bar area. Their popularity is growing – in true Viennese fashion, people embrace the new alongside the old.

Vienna is full of both types of *Beisln*. No matter which you choose, they all stay true to their roots: seasonal, regional cooking that satisfies with every bite.

KRZYSZTOF DYDYNSKI

>9 SPANISH RIDING SCHOOL

WATCH STALLIONS PRANCE TO THE TUNE OF THE WALTZ

Vienna's Lipizzaner stallions date back to the 1520s, when Ferdinand I imported the first horses from Spain for the imperial palace. Later, Archduke Charles II established the imperial stud in Lipizza (Lipica, today's Slovenia), giving the horses their name. The original baroque horses were of various colours, but it became fashionable to breed white stallions during the 19th century, when Arab and various other horses were re-introduced into the line and the horses were carefully selected.

Over the centuries, natural catastrophes, but more often war, caused the Lipizzaner to be relocated from their original stud in Slovenia on numerous occasions. Eventually, the horses were transferred to Piber, near Graz. Today, Piber still supplies the Spanish Riding School (Spanische Hofreitschule) with its white stallions.

These horses dance with a discipline and control unmatched by any other. Nothing will prepare you for their poise and magnificence. It's imperial Vienna at its most splendid. See p45 for our full review of the Spanish Riding School.

© YADID LEVY / ALAMY

>10 HOFBURG

MARVEL AT THE ULTIMATE DISPLAY OF AUSTRIA'S FORMER IMPERIAL POWER

With the Habsburgs' predilection for pomp, and with Vienna's historical roots as an imperial capital and bastion of the Occident, this was a city built to impress. And certainly not the least of it, whipped up and constantly re-vamped from the 13th century, the Hofburg forms a magnificent ensemble of architecture and museums set around historic squares. Picturesque parkland flanks it on both sides.

Home to the Habsburgs for about six centuries, this jigsaw puzzle of colossal buildings was designed to impress monarchs who visited Austria's most famous family, and to wow the masses. It's easy to feel stunned by it all. Walking around the palaces, it feels like an epic city within a city. The monumental buildings symbolise the culture and heritage of the Habsburg dynasty, who deemed no rulers should use rooms of his or her predecessor – so that each one reworked the lavish interiors. The complex spans several centuries of architecture: the oldest sections date from the 13th century; the newest from the end of the 19th.

Highlights include the Spanish Riding School (p45), where elegant horses trot their stuff; the former quarters of Sisi (Austria's illustrious empress), the Kaiserappartements (p41); the Schatzkammer (pictured below; p45); and Josefsplatz, which was named after Joseph II. The latter gained celluloid immortality in the film *The Third Man,* as it was here – outside Palais Pallavicini – that Harry Lime faked his own death.

KRZYSZTOF DYDYNSKI

>VIENNA DIARY

With so much emphasis on music and culture in Viennese life, it's fitting that most of Vienna's social calendar revolves around the arts. Opera and classical music are the mainstays, but rock-and-roll events attract just as much of a following. And then there's the ball season, with its strict dress codes and magnificent gowns. Lastly, if you're in town just before Christmas, you'll stumble into Vienna's most charming social event: the Christmas Market season.

LIFE BALL / ANDREAS TISCHLER

Flamboyant, fashionable and for a good cause: the Life Ball (p23)

VIENNA DIARY

FEBRUARY

Fasching

The Fasching season, a carnival time of costumes and parties, runs from November to Ash Wednesday, but February is traditionally when most of the action takes place. Look for street parties and drunken Viennese in silly get-ups.

Opernball

www.wiener-staatsoper.at; 01, Staatsoper

Three hundred or so balls – many of which are traditional affairs with plenty of waltzing under chandeleirs – are held during January and February's *Ballsaison* (ball season). Of them, the Opernball (Opera Ball) is number one. Held in the Staatsoper, it's a supremely lavish affair, with the men in tails and the women in shining white gowns.

MARCH & APRIL

OsterKlang Festival

www.theater-wien.at

Orchestral and chamber music recitals fill some of Vienna's best music halls during this 'Sound of Easter' festival. The highlight is the opening concert, which features the Vienna Philharmonic.

MAURIZIO BORGESE / © HEMIS / ALAMY

The Opernball: sometimes beauty is black and white

Explode with joy at Donauinselfest

© BLICKWINKEL / ALAMY

MAY & JUNE

Donauinselfest
www.donauinselfest.at
Donauinselfest is held on the Donauinsel (Danube Island) over three days on a weekend in late June. It features a feast of rock, pop, folk and country performers and attracts almost three million onlookers. Best of all, it's free!

Life Ball
www.lifeball.org
This AIDS-charity event is the unorthodox, whacky dame of the *Ballsaison* and is often graced by international celebrities. It's usually held in the Rathaus around the middle of May (though this can vary; it has been held as late as July) and sees some colourful and flamboyant outfits.

Wiener Festwochen
www.festwochen.or.at
Considered to be one of the highlights of the city's social calendar, the Vienna Festival hosts a wide-ranging arts program, based in various venues around town, from May to mid-June.

JULY & AUGUST

ImPulsTanz
www.impulstanz.com
Vienna's premier avant-garde dance festival attracts an array of internationally renowned troupes and newcomers between mid-July and mid-August. Performances are held in the MuseumsQuartier, Volkstheater and a number of small venues.

CHRISTKINDLMÄRKTE

Christkindlmärkte (Christmas markets) range from kitsch to quaint in style and atmosphere, but they all include festive crowds, loads of Christmas gifts for sale, mugs of *Glühwein* (mulled wine) and hotplates loaded with *Kartoffelpuffer* (hot potato patties) and *Maroni* (roasted chestnuts).

Some of the best take place at **Freyung** (U2 Schottentor 1A), **Rathausplatz** (1, 2) **Schönbrunn** (pictured; U4 Schönbrunn 10A) and **Spittelberg** (U2, U3 Volkstheater 49 48A). There is also a market at **Heiligenkreuzerhof** (U1, U4 Schwedenplatz), which is often forgotten, but is arguably the most authentic and quaint of all the *Christkindlmärkte*. It's off Schönlaterngasse, hidden within a residential courtyard.

ALFIO GAROZZO / CUBO IMAGES / PHOTOLIBRARY

KlangBogen Festival
www.theater-wien.at
Running from July to August, the KlangBogen Festival features operas, operettas and orchestral music in the Theater an der Wien, plus a few other locations around town.

OCTOBER
Viennale Film Festival
www.viennale.at
The country's best film festival, Viennale features fringe and independent films from around the world. It's held in October, with screenings at numerous locations.

NOVEMBER & DECEMBER
Wien Modern
www.wienmodern.at
The Wien Modern festival takes an opposing view to many of the city's music festivals by featuring modern classical and avant-garde music. The festival is held throughout November.

Christkindlmärkte
Vienna's much-loved Christmas-market season runs from mid-November to Christmas Day. See above for details.

GREG ELMS

Navigate the laneways of the World Heritage–listed Innere Stadt (p34)

ITINERARIES

Vienna is a conveniently small city with virtually all of its sights clustered in one area – the Innere Stadt. But the staggering number of things to see and the high-season, city-clogging crowds mean a bit of planning is in order if you want to make the most of your time.

DAY ONE

Start with the Stephansdom (p46) in the morning, before swinging by Graben (p38) en route to the Hofburg. The Hofburg is packed with sights; your best bet to avoid museum and church fatigue is to mix it up: try the Augustinerkirche (p35) first; followed by the Kaiserappartements and Sisi Museum (p41); and the 13th-century royal chapel, the Burgkapelle (p38); and then gape at the crown jewels in the Schatzkammer (p45). Take a stroll outside around the Burggarten (p38), a tranquil patch of green in the middle of town, and grab a drink at the Palmenhaus (p52). Finish with a casual bite at Café Drechsler (p65), which is famous for its *Gulasch*.

DAY TWO

Start the day at Naschmarkt (p86), before the crowds roll in. Next, hit the MuseumsQuartier (p56), following which you can blow out the cobwebs with a stroll around Neubau. Head back to the Naschmarkt for dinner; Neni (p91) is an excellent bet. If you've got some energy left, finish off the night with some bar-hopping through Wieden (p93) or dancing at Pratersauna (p113).

DAY THREE

Spend the morning at Schloss Schönbrunn (p117), making sure you take a walk through its spectacular gardens (see the boxed text, p118). Then hop on a tram and pay an afternoon visit to one of Mauer's exemplary *Heurigen* (p122). Head back to your hotel for a well-deserved rest before dressing up and heading out to an opera at the Staatsoper (p55) or some classical music at one of the many venues across town.

Top left Sample the exhaustive contemporary art at Kunsthalle (p58) **Top right** Complete a tourist revolution on the Riesenrad (p108) **Bottom left** Enjoy the ambience at the restored Palmenhaus (p52) **Bottom right** Designed by Otto Wagner (p151), Karlsplatz metro station is a Secessionist classic

Put your mettle to the pedal with Vienna City Bike rentals

RICHARD NEBESKY

RAINY DAY

Rain is no dampener in Vienna. Any of the churches, museums and palaces are fair game if you don't want to be out in the wet. The Muse-umsQuartier (p56) is a prime place to focus your attention, as most of its museums are clustered in one area. And when you've had your fill of history and culture, while away the afternoon at one of the city's ubiquitous cafes. Chat with your friends or just relax with a stack of reading materials (most cafes contain a selection of English newspapers). Sure you'll eat too much cake and drink too much coffee, but spending a few hours at a stalwart such as Café Sperl (p66) or Café Prückel (p50) is a quintessentially Viennese experience.

FUN FOR FREE

There's plenty of opportunity to while away a day without paying any entrance fees or cover charges. Pop into the Augustinerkirche (p35) before taking a walk around the Burggarten (p38), which will give you a good feel for the Hofburg. At noon, hop over to the Hoher Markt Ankeruhr to watch the Ankeruhr (Anker Clock; p39) procession. Then head to the Ruprechtskirche (p44). Vienna City Bike (p160) stands are scattered all

FORWARD PLANNING

Six months before you go Book tickets for the Spanische Hofreitschule (Spanish Riding School; p45).

Three months before you go Check the calendar for the Staatsoper (p55), Musikverein (p54), Kursalon (p54) and Wiener Residenzorchester (p83) and buy tickets for anything that looks appealing.

Three weeks before you go Book a table at Meinl am Graben (p49) or Österreicher im Mak (p50).

One week before you go Buy tickets for Schloss Schönbrunn (p117).

over the city and the first hour is free, so keep an eye out and take a short spin. Finish off the day at the Naschmarkt (p86), but be forewarned: while a stroll through the stalls costs zero, we can't guarantee you won't be tempted by its culinary treasures.

UNDERGROUND

Ride Vienna's trams (p160) and get your budget back on track

KRZYSZTOF DYDYNSKI

NEIGHBOURHOODS

Vienna's topography is like a lake with concentric ripples washing out from its centre. The stone that first set those ripples in motion was cast by the Romans, who created a military outpost here. Later, city planners carved the lake up into 23 numbered districts, each of which has its own unique character and flair.

The city centre (the Innere Stadt) is encircled by the Ringstrasse (Ring Road), which was once a sloped clearing forming part of the city's 13th-century fortifications. Moving outwards, wedged between the Ringstrasse and the next major circular road, the Gürtel, are the high-density *Vorstädte* (inner suburbs). Beyond the *Vorstädte* are the *Vororte* (suburbs), which give way in the north and west to the *Heuriger*-filled Wienerwald (Vienna Woods). Generally, the higher the district number, the further it is from the centre.

The Innere Stadt (district 01) is a Unesco-listed site filled with architectural masterpieces, from the medieval to the postmodern, and everything in between. Neubau (07) boasts the culture-packed MuseumsQuartier, and joins neighbouring Mariahilf (06), Wieden (04) and Margareten (05) in a lively ribbon south and west of the centre. These areas are experiencing gentrification as more-affluent Viennese move in. Outside the Gürtel, Schloss Schönbrunn and Hietzing (13) are gloriously upmarket.

Northwest and north of the centre, the area encompassing Josefstadt (08) and Alsergrund (09) has a lively university campus and some quality sights, such as Palais Liechtenstein (Liechtenstein Museum). Our Belvedere to the Canal chapter covers Landstrasse (03), which hugs the Danube Canal southeast of the Innere Stadt. The main attractions here are the magnificent Belvedere Palace (Schloss Belvedere) and Hundertwasserhaus.

East of the Innere Stadt, across the Danube Canal, is Leopoldstadt (02), a Middle Ages Jewish quarter. Up and coming and begging discovery, it's also home to the Riesenrad (giant Ferris wheel). Further east lies green Donaupark and Donaustadt, home to Vienna's UN contingent.

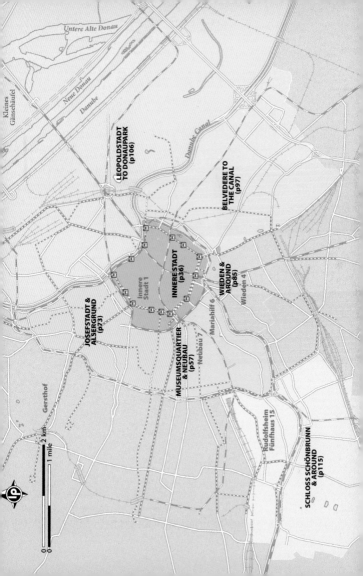

Untere Alte Donau

Kleines Gänsehäufel

Neue Donau

Danube

LEOPOLDSTADT
TO DONAUPARK
(p106)

Danube Canal

BELVEDERE TO
THE CANAL
(p97)

Innere
Stadt 1

INNERE STADT
(p36)

WIEDEN &
AROUND
(p85)

JOSEFSTADT &
ALSERGRUND
(p73)

Mariahilf 6

Wieden 4

MUSEUMSQUARTIER
& NEUBAU
(p57)

Neubau 7

Gersthof

Rudolfsheim
Fünfhaus 15

SCHLOSS SCHÖNBRUNN
& AROUND
(p115)

0   2 km
0   1 mile

INNERE STADT

Vienna's most sights-packed area, the Innere Stadt (inner city) is also the oldest part of Austria's capital and a Unesco World Heritage Site. Round and dense, most of its attractions are found within the Ringstrasse (Ring Road). The area bubbles over with high-profile culture, starting in its southeast with the Kunsthistorisches and Naturhistorisches Museums and the Hofburg, the ultimate display of Austria's former imperial power. This district was once home to the Habsburg rulers and includes (among other key sights) the Spanish Riding School (Spanische Hofreitschule) and the Kaiserapartements. Moving clockwise, the Rathaus sits outside

INNERE STADT

Please see over for map

the Ringstrasse on the district's western edge and the Danube skims its northeastern side. Continuing south you hit the Stadtpark, to the southwest, followed by the Staatsoper. The colourful Stephansdom sits firmly in the Innere Stadt's centre, and the area is peppered with dozens more sights and some of Vienna's most prominent restaurants and shops.

SEE

ALBERTINA
☎ 534 83-0; www.albertina.at; 01, Helmut-Zilk-Platz 1; adult/under 19yr €9.50/free; ⏱ 10am-6pm Thu-Tue, to 9pm Wed; ⊕ U1, U2, U4 Karlsplatz 🚌 3A

Once used as the Habsburgs' imperial apartments for guests, the Albertina now houses the greatest collection of graphic art in the world. An astonishing 1.5 million prints and 50,000 drawings, including 145 Dürer drawings (the largest collection in the world), 43 by Raphael, 70 by Rembrandt and 150 by Schiele.

AUGUSTINERKIRCHE
☎ 533 70 99; 01, Augustinerstrasse 3; admission free; ⊕ U1, U3 Herrengasse 🚌 2A, 3A

The Augustinerkirche (Augustinian Church) is most famous for being where the hearts of 54 Habsburg rulers are kept. The urns can be viewed in the **Herzgrüftel** (Little Heart Crypt; tour adult/child €2.50/1.75; ⏱ approx 12.30pm Sun, following mass, other days by appointment). The church also hosts regular evening classical-music concerts, and the 11am Mass on

Sunday is celebrated with a full choir and orchestra.

BEETHOVEN PASQUALATIHAUS
☎ 535 89 05; 01, Mölker Bastei 8; adult/under 19yr/concession €2/free/1; ⏱ 10am-1pm & 2-6pm Tue-Sun; ⊕ U2 Schottentor 🚌 37, 38, 40-44

Between 1804 and 1814 Beethoven lived and composed symphonies 4, 5 and 7 and the opera *Fidelio*, among other works, at this address. A small collection of photos, articles and a handful of his personal belongings are on display.

VIENNA'S RINGSTRASSE
The Ringstrasse, or the Ring as it's known locally, is a wide, tree-lined boulevard encircling much of the Innere Stadt along the line of the former 16th-century city walls. These walls originally had the extra protection of a ditch or moat, and defenders could hurl heavy stuff at their exposed invaders on the wide, sloped clearing beyond. Anyone living in the *Vorstädte* (inner suburbs) outside the fortress was expected to flee inside as invading forces approached – or take their chances outside.

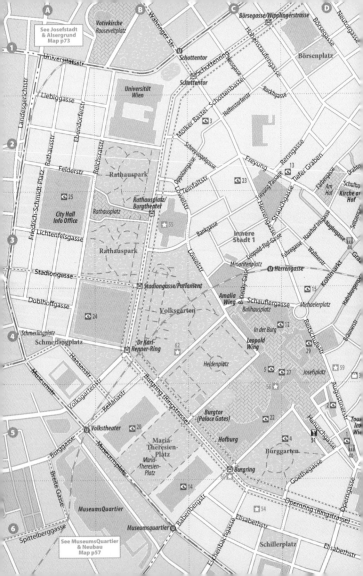

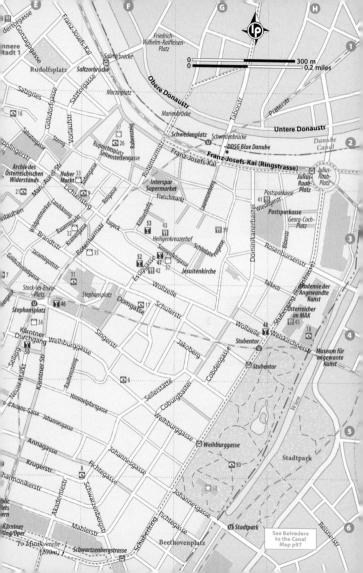

🅒 BURGGARTEN

01, Burgring; admission free; 🕑 6am-10pm Apr-Oct, to 8pm Nov-Mar; 🚇 U2 Museumsquartier, U2, U3 Volkstheater 🚋 D, 1, 2 🚌 2A, 57A

Tucked behind the Hofburg, the Burggarten (Castle Garden) is a leafy oasis amid the hustle and bustle of the Ringstrasse and Innere Stadt. The marble statue of Mozart is the park's most famous tenant, but there's also a statue of Franz Josef in military garb.

🅒 BURGKAPELLE

☎ 533 99 27; www.hofburgkapelle.at, in German; 01, Schweizerhof; admission €1.50; 🕑 11am-3pm Mon-Thu, to 1pm Fri; 🚇 U3 Herrengasse 🚌 2A, 3A

The Burgkapelle (Royal Chapel) originally dates from the 13th century. It received a Gothic makeover from 1447 to 1449, but much of this disappeared during the baroque fad. The vaulted wooden statuary survives and is testament to those Gothic days. This is where the **Vienna Boys' Choir Mass** (see the boxed text, p54) takes place, every Sunday at 9.15am from September to June. The chapel is sometimes closed to visitors in July and August, so check ahead in those months.

🅒 FRANZISKANERKIRCHE

☎ 512 45 7811; 01, Franziskanerplatz; admission free; 🕑 7am-8pm; 🚇 U1, U3 Stephansplatz

This Franciscan church is a glorious architectural deception. Viewed from outside, it exudes all the hallmarks of early 17th-century Renaissance style, yet inside it is awash with gold and marble decorative features from the baroque era about 100 years later.

🅒 GRABEN

01; 🚇 U1, U3 Stephansplatz

Graben literally began life as a ditch dug by the Romans to protect Vindobona. In 1192 Leopold V filled in their ditch and built a

---

HOFBURG

The Hofburg is a jigsaw puzzle of absurdly monumental buildings. Home to the Habsburg rulers from Rudolph I in 1279 until the Austrian monarchy collapsed under Karl I in 1918, it was designed particularly to impress monarchs visiting Austria's most famous family.

Today the Hofburg houses the offices of the Austrian president and an ensemble of extraordinary museums and sights set around historic squares, flanked by parkland on both sides. The **Spanish Riding School** (p45), the **Schatzkammer** (p45), and the **Kaiserappartements** (p41), the former imperial apartments of the Habsburgs, are all found here, together with the **Albertina** (p35), **Augustinerkirche** (p35), **Burgkapelle** (above), **Neue Burg Museums** (p43) and the **Kunsthistorisches Museum** (p41).

A treat for time travellers, the Ankeruhr RICHARD NEBESKY

defensive city wall that ended in Freyung. He financed the project with the ransom paid by arch-rival Richard the Lionheart, who at that time was being kept under lock and key in a castle near Dürnstein, on the Danube. Two fascinating landmarks on this street are the writhing, towering **Pestsäule** (Plague Column), and **Adolf Loos' public toilets**, which are in the *Jugendstil* (art nouveau) design. The withering, towering Pestsäule commemorates the end of the plague and was erected in 1692. It was designed by Johann Bernhard Fischer von Erlach – don't miss this, as it is one of the finest monuments in Europe.

ANKERUHR

Named after the Anker Insurance Co, the **Ankeruhr** (Anker Clock; 01; Hoher Markt; 🚇 U1, U3 Stephansplatz; 🚌 1A, 2A 3A) is an art nouveau masterpiece. Over a 12-hour period, figures slowly pass across the clock face, indicating the time against a static measure showing the minutes. Figures represented range from Joseph Haydn to Maria Theresia. Everyone flocks here at noon, when the figures trundle past all at once in succession and organ music is piped out.

🎵 HAUS DER MUSIK

☎ 516 48-0; www.hdm.at; 01, Seilerstätte 30; adult/under 12yr €10/5.50; ⏰ 10am-10pm; 🚋 1, 2 🚌 3A
The Haus der Musik explains sounds in an amusing and interactive way. Listen to a shortened version of the world-famous Vienna Philharmonic New Year's concert, play with an interactive tool that allows you to compose your own waltz with the roll of a dice or play around with sampled sounds to record your own CD (€7).

🎵 HELMUT-ZILK-PLATZ (ALBERTINAPLATZ)

01; 🚇 U1, U3 Stephansplatz, U4 Karlsplatz
This square is the site of the troubling work **Monument against War & Fascism** by Alfred Hrdlicka. The

series of pale blocklike sculptures commemorates Jews and other victims of war and fascism. The dark, squat shape wrapped in barbed wire represents a Jew scrubbing the floor; the greyish block originally came from the Mauthausen concentration camp.

HOLOCAUST-DENKMAL

01, Judenplatz; 2A, 3A

The Holocaust-Denkmal, a memorial to the 65,000 Austrian Jews who perished in the Holocaust, is the focal point of Judenplatz. The pale, bulky sculpture is in the shape of a library where the books' spines face inwards, and has the names of Austrian concentration camps written across its base. It represents the untold stories of Holocaust victims.

JÜDISCHES MUSEUM

☎ 535 04 31; www.jmw.at; 01, Dorotheergasse 11; adult/child €6.50/4; ⏰ 10am-6pm Sun-Fri; ☻ U1, U3 Stephansplatz

Occupying three floors of Palais Eskeles, Vienna's Jüdisches Museum uses holograms and an assortment of objects to document the history of Jewish people in Vienna, from the first settlements at Judenplatz in the 13th century through to the present. Temporary exhibitions are a key feature of the museum.

The Holocaust-Denkmal, a library of untold stories

RICHARD NEBESKY

KAISERAPPARTEMENTS
☎ 533 75 70; www.hofburg-wien.at; 01, Innerer Burghof, Kaisertor; adult/under 19yr/student €9.90/5.90/8.90; ⏲ 9am-5.30pm Sep-Jun, to 6pm Jul & Aug; Ⓤ U3 Herrengasse 🚌 2A, 3A

The Kaiserappartements (Imperial Apartments) were once the official living quarters of Franz Josef I and Empress Elisabeth (or Sisi, as she was affectionately known). The first section is known as the **Sisi Museum** and is devoted to Austria's most beloved empress. Clothing and jewellery dominate, though many of the empress's famous portraits are also on show.

KUNSTFORUM
☎ 537 33 26; www.bankaustria-kunstforum.at; 01, Freyung 8; adult/17-27yr/senior/family €9/6/7.50/20; ⏲ 10am-7pm Sat-Thu, to 9pm Fri; Ⓤ U3 Herrengasse 🚌 2A, 3A

The Kunstforum museum stages an exciting program of changing exhibitions that focus on a specific theme, often with a modern skew. One in recent years focused on food in still-life art, with 90 works from the 16th to the 20th centuries, some by Cézanne and Picasso.

KUNSTHISTORISCHES MUSEUM
☎ 525 24-0; www.khm.at; 01, Maria-Theresien-Platz; adult/under 19yr €12/ free; ⏲ 10am-6pm Tue, Wed & Fri-Sun, to 9pm Thu; Ⓤ U2 Museumsquartier 🚋 D, 1, 2

This art-history museum brims with works by Europe's finest painters, sculptors and artisans (although it was closed for long-term restoration at the time of publication). The Picture Gallery offers a breathtaking window into mainly Flemish, Dutch, Italian and German works from the 16th and 17th centuries – the time when the Habsburgs went on a collecting frenzy.

LOOS HAUS
01, Michaelerplatz 3; ⏲ 8am or 9am-3pm Mon-Wed & Fri, 9am-5.30pm Thu; Ⓤ U1, U3 Stephansplatz

Designed by Adolf Loos, the intentionally simple facade of this modernist gem offended emperor Franz Josef so deeply that he ordered the curtains be closed on all palace windows overlooking the building. Critics dubbed it a 'house without eyebrows', referring to its lack of window detail, and eventually Loos agreed to add 10 window boxes.

MARIA AM GESTADE
☎ 533 9594-0; http://maria-am-gestade.redemptoristen.at, in German; 01, Passauer Platz; Ⓤ U1, U3 Stephansplatz 🚌 1A, 2A, 3A

Originally a wooden church, today Maria am Gestade (Maria on the

Riverbank) is a shapely, Gothic beauty of stone. Because of the steep ground, the nave was built narrower than the choir (and with a slight bend). When Napoleon came to town from 1805, he used it as a store for his weapons and stall for his horses. The interior, with its high vaulted Gothic ceiling and pretty stained glass behind a winged Gothic altar, can only be viewed during services.

🇨 MOZARTHAUS VIENNA

☎ 512 17 91; www.mozarthausvienna.at; 01, Domgasse 5; adult/concession & under 14yr €9/7; ⏱ 10am-7pm; 🚇 U1, U3 Stephansplatz 🚌 1A

The residence where the great composer penned *The Marriage of Figaro* is worth a visit for an insight into the life and times of Mozart in Vienna. His vices – womanising, gambling and his ability to waste excessive amounts of money – lend a spicy edge (note the peepholes).

🇨 MUSEUM FÜR ANGEWANDTE KUNST

☎ 711 360; www.mak.at; 01, Stubenring 5; adult/under 19yr €7.90/free, Sat free; ⏱ 10am-6pm Wed-Sun, to midnight Tue; 🚇 U3 Stubentor 🚌 2

Better known as the MAK, the Museum of Applied Arts is an extensive collection of household items. Renaissance, baroque, oriental, historicist, empire, art deco and the distinctive metalwork of the *Wiener Werkstätte* (Vienna Workshop) all feature here. Don't miss the cafe **Österreicher im MAK** (p50).

🇨 MUSEUM JUDENPLATZ

☎ 535 04 31; www.jmw.at; 01, Judenplatz 8; adult €4; ⏱ 10am-6pm Sun-Thu, to 2pm Fri; 🚌 2A, 3A

The main focus of the city's second Jewish museum is the excavated remains of a medieval synagogue that once stood on Judenplatz. Built around 1420, it didn't last long: Duke Albrecht V ordered its destruction in 1421. The basic outline of the synagogue can still be seen, lit with subdued lighting. A small model of the building completes the picture.

🇨 NATURHISTORISCHES MUSEUM

☎ 521 77-0; www.nhm-wien.ac.at; 01, Burgring 7; adult/under 19yr/student €10/free/5; ⏱ 9am-6.30pm Thu-Mon, to 9pm Wed; 🚇 U2, U3 Volkstheater 🚌 D, 1, 2

Exhibits on minerals, meteorites and assorted animal remains in jars, as well as some fascinating Stone Age Venus figurines, dominate here. Two 'must-sees' are the 25,000-year-old statuette *Venus of Willendorf* and the 32,000 BC statuette original *Dancing Fanny* (the oldest figurative sculpture in the world).

◎ NEIDHART-FRESKEN

☎ 535 90 65; 01, Tuchlauben 19; adult/child/student/senior €6/free/3/4; ⏱ 10am-1pm & 2-6pm Tue, 2-6pm Fri-Sun; 🚌 2A, 3A

An unassuming house on Tuch-lauben hides some quite remark-able decoration: the oldest extant secular murals in Vienna. The small frescoes, dating from 1398, tell the story of the minstrel Neidhart von Reuental (1180–1240) and life in the Middle Ages in lively and jolly scenes.

◎ NEUE BURG MUSEUMS

☎ 525 24-0; 01, Heldenplatz; adult/un-der 19yr/concession €12/free/9; ⏱ 10am-6pm Wed-Sun; 🚋 D, 1, 2 🚌 2A

You get three museums in one at the Neue Burg. Instruments of all shapes and sizes fill the **Sammlung Alter Musikinstrumente**. The **Ephesos Museum** contains artefacts from Ephesus and Samothrace donated (some say 'lifted') by the Sultan in 1900 after a team of Austrian archaeologists excavated the famous site in Turkey. And the **Hofjagd und Rüstkammer** collection features superb examples of 15th- and 16th-century armour.

◎ PALAIS KINSKY

01, Freyung 4; ⏱ 10am-6pm Mon-Fri; Ⓤ U2 Schottentor 🚌 1A

Palais Kinsky has a classic baroque facade, but its highlight is an elaborate three-storey stairway off to the left of the first inner courtyard; it has elegant banisters graced with statues at every turn. The ceiling fresco is a fanciful creation filled with podgy cherubs, bare-breasted beauties and the occasional strongman.

◎ PARLAMENT

☎ 401 10 2400; www.parlament.gv.at; 01, Dr-Karl-Renner-Ring 3; tours adult/under 19yr/concession €4/1/2; Ⓤ U2, U3 Volkstheater 🚋 D, 1, 2, 46, 49

The Parlament building opposite the Volksgarten strikes a governing pose over the Ringstrasse. Its neo-classical facade and Greek pillars, designed by Theophil von Hansen in 1883, are striking. The beautiful **Athena Fountain**, sculpted by Carl Kundmann, guards the building and offsets it magnificently.

◎ RATHAUS

☎ 525 50; www.wien.gv.at; 01, Rathausplatz; ⏱ tours 1pm Mon, Wed & Fri; Ⓤ U2 Rathaus 🚋 D, 1, 2

This neo-Gothic concoction, completed in 1883 by Friedrich von Schmidt, was modelled on Flemish city halls. Its main spire soars to 102m, if you include the pennant held by the knight at the top. You're free to wander through the seven inner court-yards, but you must join a guided tour (free) to see the interior,

NEIGHBOURHOODS

INNERE STADT

The Rathaus (p43), a towering Flemish-Gothic masterpiece

RICHARD NEBESKY

which has red carpets, gigantic mirrors and frescoes. The largest of the courtyards occasionally hosts concerts.

🅒 RÖMER MUSEUM

☎ 535 56 06; 01, Hoher Markt 3; adult/under 19yr/concession €4/free/3; 🕙 9am-6pm Tue-Sun; Ⓜ U1, U3 Stephansplatz 🚌 1A, 2A, 3A

Who knows what the Romans would make of their former outpost today being hidden beneath a restaurant on Hoher Markt? This small expanse of Roman ruins dating from the 1st to the 5th century are thought to be part of the officers' quarters of the Roman legion camp at Vindobona. You can

see crumbled walls and tiled floors, and a small but selective exhibit on artefacts found during the excavations. The ruins are part of the Wien Museum – a municipal museum ensemble.

🅒 RUPRECHTSKIRCHE

☎ 535 60 03; www.ruprechtskirche. at, in German; 01, Seitenstettengasse 5; free; 🕙 10am-noon Mon-Fri & 3-5pm Mon, Wed & Fri; Ⓜ U1, U3 Stephansplatz 🚌 1A, 2A, 3A

A few steps north of Ruprechtsplatz, Ruprechtskirche (St Rupert's Church) dates from about 1137, or earlier, making it the oldest church in Vienna. The lower levels of the tower date from the

11th century, the roof from the 15th century and the iron Renaissance door on the west side from the 1530s. What makes this church attractive is its unusually simple exterior of ivy-clad stone walls in cobblestoned surrounds. The interior is just as sleek and worth viewing, with a Romanesque nave from the 12th century.

SCHATZKAMMER

☎ 525 24-0; www.khm.at; 01, Schweizerhof; adult/child under 19 €12/free; 10am-6pm Wed-Mon; U3 Herrengasse, 2A, 3A

The secular and ecclesiastical treasures of priceless value and splendour, and the sheer wealth of this collection of crown jewels in the Imperial Treasury, are staggering. As you walk through the rooms you will see a golden rose, a 2680-carat Colombian emerald and – the highlight of the treasury – the imperial crown.

SECESSION

☎ 587 53 07; www.secession.at; 01, Friedrichstrasse 12; exhibition & frieze adult/concession €8.50/5, exhibition only €5/4; 10am-6pm Tue-Sun; U1, U2, U4 Karlsplatz

In 1897, 19 progressive artists broke away from the Künstlerhaus and the conservative artistic establishment it represented and formed the Vienna Secession (Sezession). Their aim was to present current trends in contemporary art and shake off historicism. Among their number were Gustav Klimt, Josef Hoffman, Kolo Moser and Joseph M Olbrich (a former student of Wagner). Olbrich designed this exhibition centre of the Secessionists, which combines sparse functionality with stylistic motifs.

The building's most striking feature is a delicate golden dome rising from a turret on the roof that deserves better than the 'golden cabbage' description accorded it by some Viennese. Other features are the Medusa-like faces above the door with dangling serpents instead of ear lobes, minimalist stone owls gazing down from the walls and vast ceramic pots supported by tortoises at the front.

SPANISH RIDING SCHOOL

☎ 533 90 31; www.srs.at; 01, Michaelerplatz 1; performances €23-143; U3 Herrengasse 2A, 3

The Spanish Riding School (Spanische Hofreitschule) is a Viennese institution truly reminiscent of the imperial Habsburg era. This unequalled equestrian show is performed by Lipizzaner stallions formerly kept at an imperial stud established at Lipizza (hence 'Lipizzaner'), now within Slovenia and known as Lipica. Today the stud is in the Austrian region of Styria. These graceful stallions perform an equine ballet to a program of classical music beneath shimmering chandeliers. You need to plan ahead if you want to attend: tickets sell out months beforehand. If you don't manage to snag a ticket, check out the morning training sessions (see the website for times).

☉ STADTPARK

01, 03; ☉ U4 Stadtpark, ◻ D
The Stadtpark (City Park) is an enjoyable recreational spot with winding paths and a pond. Of the several statues inhabiting the park (including Schindler, Bruckner and Schubert), the most recognisable is the golden **Johann Strauss Denkmal**.

☉ STEPHANSDOM

☎ 515 52 3540; www.stephanskirche. at; 01, Stephansplatz; admission free; ☽ 6am-10pm Mon-Sat, from 7am Sun; ☉ U1, U3 Stephansplatz
Vienna's Gothic masterpiece, Stephansdom (St Stephan's Cathedral), or Steffl (Little Stephan), is like no other. The glorious tiled roof, with its dazzling row of chevrons on one end and the Austrian eagle on the other, mesmerises even the most cathedral-jaded traveller. Inside, a magnificent Gothic stone pulpit

fashioned in 1515 by Anton Pilgram takes pride of place. One often overlooked detail is the pulpit's handrail, which has salamanders and toads fighting an eternal battle of good versus evil up and down its length. The baroque high altar, at the very far end of the nave, shows the stoning of St Stephan.

🛍 SHOP

🛍 ART UP *Fashion, Accessories*

☎ 535 50 97; www.artup.at; 01, Bauernmarkt 8; ☽ 11.30am-6.30pm Mon-Fri, 11am-5pm Sat; ☉ U1, U3 Stephansplatz
Take the temperature of Vienna's contemporary design scene at Art Up, a cooperative allowing the designers who stock their work here to get a foothold in the fashion world. Elegant fashion pieces rub alongside quirky accessories (Astroturf tie or handbag, anyone?) as well as ceramics and bigger art pieces.

🛍 AUSTRIAN DELIGHTS
Food, Gifts

☎ 532 16 61; www.austriandelights .at; 01, Judengasse 1a; ☽ 11am-7pm Mon-Fri, to 6pm Sat; ☉ U1, U3 Stephansplatz
Stocking Austrian-made items by mainly small producers, you'll find regional specialities – fine confectionery, local wine, schnapps,

cognac, jams, jellies, chutneys, honey, vinegars and oils – that you can't find anywhere else in the capital. Most of it is, as the owner says, 'items Austrian grandmothers make'.

MANNER *Food, Gifts*

☎ 513 70 18; www.manner.com; 01, Stephansplatz 7; ⏰ 10am-9pm Sun-Fri, 9.30am-8.30pm Sat; ⓜ U1, U3 Stephansplatz

Vienna's favourite sweet since 1898, a glorious concoction of wafers and hazelnut cream, Manner has its own concept store, now decked out in the biscuit's signature peachy pink. Buy the product in every imaginable vari-

ety and packaging combination. It's a fab snack to carry around sightseeing.

ÖSTERREICHISCHE WERKSTÄTTEN
Glassware & Porcelain

☎ 512 24 18; www.austrianarts. com; 01, Kärntner Strasse 6; ⏰ 10am-6.30pm Mon-Fri, to 6pm Sat; ⓜ U1, U3 Stephansplatz

Established in 1945, Österreich-ische Werkstätten is dedicated to selling work designed by Austrian designers and made by Austrian companies. Look out for Kisslinger, a family glassware company established in 1946, with Klimt- and Hundertwasser-styled designs; and

Shoppers turn glassy-eyed at Österreichische Werkstätten

KRZYSZTOF DYDYNSKI

ALTWAREN AUCTIONS

You may never dream of dropping into Sotheby's, but when in Vienna it's perfectly natural to inspect what's on offer at the **Dorotheum** (☎ 515 60-0; www.dorotheum.com; 01, Dorotheergasse 17; ⏱ 10am-6pm Mon-Fri, 9am-5pm Sat; Ⓜ 2A, 3A). Among the largest auction houses in Europe, this is the apex of Vienna's *Altwaren*-consumer culture, the *Flohmarkt's* (flea market) wealthy uncle. Something between a museum and the fanciest car-boot sale you ever saw, rooms are filled with everything from antique toys and tableware to autographs, antique guns and Old Masters paintings.

Affordable household ornaments are up for grabs among pricier ones. Auction proceedings are fun to watch even if you don't intend to buy, and you can purchase items at marked prices in the Freier Verkauf section.

the world-renowned Riedel wine glasses.

🛍 VIENNA BAG *Accessories*
☎ 513 11 84; 01, www.vienna-bag.com; Bäckerstrasse 7; ⏱ 10.30am-6pm Mon-Fri, to 5pm Sat

Vienna Bag has been making funky and practical handbags and satchels since 2001. In both black and brightly coloured varieties, they're strong, lightweight and washable, as well as chic.

🍴 EAT

🍴 AUBERGINE
French, Austrian   €€€
☎ 968 31 83; 01, Gonzagagasse 14; 3-course business lunch €21.50, mains €21-24, 3-5 course evening menus €42-62; ⏱ 11.30am-2.30pm & 6pm-midnight Mon-Fri year-round, 6pm-midnight Sat Dec; Ⓤ U2 Schottentor Ⓣ 1

Aubergine greets you with its namesake, a delicate slither of

salted, marinated eggplant to whet the appetite. After that it leads you into a culinary wonderland that might include *Kalbsbeuschel,* thin slices of offal garnished with snail caviar (it's less salty than sturgeon caviar and doesn't explode as easily when you bite on it) for €16.80.

🍴 BEIM CZAAK
Beisl   €
☎ 513 72 15; 01, Postgasse 15; midday menu €6.90-7.90, mains €8-16.50; ⏱ 11am-midnight Mon-Sat; Ⓤ U1, U4 Schwedenplatz Ⓣ 1, 2

In contrast to more heavily touristed *Beisln* (small taverns) in the Innere Stadt, Beim Czaak has a genuine and relatively simple interior. As you would expect, meat dishes dominate the menu, with choices such as *Waldviertler Schnitzel* (with fried bacon, onions and mushrooms) and the *Haus Schnitzel* (weighted down with ham, cheese, mushrooms and onions – yum!).

🍴 BITZINGER WÜRSTEL-STAND AM ALBERTINAPLATZ

Sausage Stand   €

01, Albertinaplatz; sausages €2.80-3.50; 🕙 10am-4am Nov-Mar, 24hr Apr-Oct; Ⓜ U1, U2, U4 Karlsplatz 🚋 D, 1, 2, 62
Located behind the Staatsoper, Vienna's best and most famous sausage stand offers the contrasting spectacle of ladies and gents dressed to the nines, enjoying a sausage, with Moët & Chandon or Stiegl Goldbräu beer.

🍴 EXPEDIT *Italian*   €€

☎ 512 33 13 23; 01, Wiesingerstrasse 6; mains €8-25; 🕙 10am-1am Mon-Sat, to 10pm Sun; 🚋 1, 2
Expedit has successfully moulded itself on a Ligurian *Osteria* (an Italian-style eatery, similar to a tavern) and become one of the most popular Italian restaurants in town. Its warehouse decor – with shelves stocked full of oil, pesto, olives and wine from Liguria – helps to create a busy yet informal atmosphere and a clean, smart look.

🍴 FIGLMÜLLER *Beisl*   €€

☎ 512 61 77; 01, Wollzeile 5; mains €7-15; 🕙 11am-10.30pm Sep-Jul; 🚍 1A
Vienna, and the Viennese, would simply be at a loss without

Figlmüller. This famous *Beisl* has some of the biggest – and best – schnitzels in the business. It's closed during August.

🍴 HOLLMANN SALON

Neo-Beisl   €€

☎ 961 19 60 40; www.hollman-salon.at; 01, Grashofgasse 3; mains €14-19, 3-4-course menus €29-39; 🕙 noon-3pm & 6-10pm Mon-Sat, from 10am Sat; Ⓜ U1, U3 Stephansplatz, U3 Stubentor 🚋 71; ✂ 📶 Ⓥ
Hollmann Salon combines the rural flavour of a country homestead with urban chic. Its succulent organic meats come from the Waldviertel north of the Danube and its menu changes every month, ensuring the very best of seasonal produce from local producers.

🍴 MEINL AM GRABEN

International   €€€

☎ 532 33 34; www.meinlamgraben.at; 01, Graben 19; mains from €30, 3-course menu €35; 🕙 8am-midnight Mon-Fri, from 9am Sat; Ⓜ U1, U3 Stephansplatz 🚍 1A, 2A, 3A; Ⓥ
Meinl am Graben combines cuisine of superlative quality with an unrivalled wine list and views of Graben. The head chef, Joachim Gradwohl, uses the freshest ingredients to create inviting dishes, often integrating delicate Mediterranean sauces and sweet aromas.

Meinl am Graben (p49): delicate sauces, sweet aromas

KRZYSZTOF DYDYNSKI

🍴 ÖSTERREICHER IM MAK

Austrian €€

☎ 7140 121; 01, Stubenring 5; lunch
special €6.40, mains €14.50-20.80;
🕐 8.30-1am; 🚇 U3 Stubentor
🚋 1, 2

Located in the Museum für
Angewandte Kunst (p42), Österreicher im MAK is the brainchild
of Helmut Österreicher, one of the
country's leading chefs and a force
behind the movement towards
back-to-the-roots Austrian fla-
vours. He enhances classic dishes
such as *Tafelspitz* (prime boiled
beef) with exotic ingredients.
Sleek interior architectural lines
create a modern flourish.

50

🍸 DRINK

🍸 AIDA *Coffee House*

☎ 512 29 77; 01, Stock-im-Eisen-Platz 2;
🕐 7am-8pm Mon-Sat, from 9am Sun;
🚇 U1, U3 Stephansplatz

An icon of the *Konditorei* (cake
shop) scene, Aida is a time warp
for coffee lovers. Its pink-and-
brown colour scheme – right
down to the waitresses' socks –
matches the 1950s retro decor
perfectly, and most of the clientele are well into retirement.

🍸 CAFÉ ALT WIEN
Coffee House

☎ 512 52 22; 01, Bäckerstrasse 9;
🕐 10am-2am Sun-Thu, to 3am Fri & Sat;
🚇 U1, U3 Stephansplatz 🚋 1A, 2A; 📶

Dark, bohemian and full of
character, Alt Wien is a classic
dive attracting students and arty
types. It's also a one-stop shop for
the low-down on events in the
city – all available wall space is
plastered with posters advertising
shows, concerts and exhibitions.
The *Gulasch* (goulash) is legendary and perfectly complemented
by dark bread and beer.

🍸 CAFÉ PRÜCKEL *Coffee House*

☎ 512 61 15; 01, Stubenring 24;
🕐 8.30am-10pm; 🚇 U3 Stubentor
🚋 1, 2

Prückel's mould is a little different
from other Viennese cafes: instead
of a sumptuous interior, it features

Christian Schnakl,
Waiter at Café Sacher (p52), home of Vienna's famous Sachertorte.

What makes the Sachertorte so special? The fact that it is still made according to the original, very secret recipe. The chocolate is so delicate yet full of flavour. That paired with the thin centre of jam makes it endlessly satisfying. Plus, you sample it in such regal and decadent surrounds, and you can even take an entire torte home, if you like. **What makes Vienna so magical?** It's so relaxing yet full of so much culture. But it also has enough energy and multicultural communities, so it never feels boring. **Where do you recommend people go to walk off that slice of cake?** A stroll through the Stadtpark (p46), where you can meander past statues of famous composers like Johann Strauss. **Where do you go on your day off?** To one of Vienna's *Heurigen* – there are so many! Everyone will find a favourite, or three.

NEIGHBOURHOODS

INNERE STADT

an intact 1950s design. Intimate booths, aloof waiters, strong coffee and diet-destroying cakes are all attractions. Live piano is played 7pm to 10pm Monday, Wednesday and Friday.

☿ CAFÉ SACHER Coffee House

☎ 541 56-0; 01, Philharmonikerstrasse 4; ☼ 8am-11.30pm; ⊕ U1, U2, U4 Karlsplatz ⬚ D, 1, 2 ⬚ 59A, 62

Sacher is the cafe every second tourist wants to visit. Why? Because of the celebrated Sachertorte (€4), a rich chocolate cake with apricot jam, once favoured by Emperor Franz Josef. Truth be told, as cafes go Sacher doesn't rate highly for authenticity, but it

pleases with its opulent furnishings, battalion of waiters and air of nobility.

☿ KRUGER'S AMERICAN BAR
Cocktail Bar

☎ 512 24 55; 01, Krugerstrasse 5; ☼ 7pm-4am Thu-Sat, to 2am Sun-Wed; ⊕ U1, U2, U4 Karlsplatz ⬚ D, 1, 2 ⬚ 59A, 62

Wood-panelled walls, tuxedoed waiters and low lighting define this throwback as a 1920 gentlemen's club. Sip martinis or top-shelf whiskey while you recline in your exquisite leather armchair in this old-world charmer.

☿ LOOS AMERICAN BAR
Cocktail Bar

☎ 512 32 83; 01, Kärntner Durchgang 10; ☼ noon-4am Sun-Wed, to 5am Thu-Sat; ⊕ U1, U3 Stephansplatz

Loos is *the* spot for a classic cocktail in the Innere Stadt, expertly whipped up by talented mixologists. Designed by Adolf Loos in 1908, this tiny box is covered head to toe in onyx and polished brass, and mirrored walls trick the mind into thinking it's a far bigger space. Beware: gawkers popping in only for a glimpse of the interior will be swiftly ejected.

☿ PALMENHAUS Bar, Cafe

☎ 533 10 33; 01, Burggarten; ☼ 10am-2am Mar-Oct, reduced hrs & closed Mon &

Loos American Bar – find a good time KRZYSZTOF DYDYNSKI

Tue Jan & Feb; Ⓜ U1, U2, U4 Karlsplatz 🚊 D, 1, 2 🚌 59A, 62

Housed in a beautifully restored Victorian palm house, complete with high, arched ceilings, glass walls and steel beams, Palmenhaus occupies one of the most attractive locations in Vienna. The crowd is generally well-to-do, but the ambience is relaxed and welcoming.

🍸 VIS-A-VIS
Wine Bar

☎ 512 93 50; 01, Wollzeile 5; ⏱ 4.30-10.30pm Tue-Sat; 🚌 1A

This wee wine bar is hidden down a narrow, atmospheric passage, directly across from famed *Beisl* Figlmüller (p49). It may only seat about 10, but it makes up for it with more than 350 wines on offer (with a strong emphasis on Austrian faves).

🍸 ZWÖLF APOSTELKELLER
Stadtheuriger

☎ 512 67 77; 01, Sonnenfelsgasse 3; ⏱ 11am-midnight; U1, U3 Stephansplatz 🚌 1A

Even though Zwölf Apostelkeller (Twelve Apostle Cellar) plays it up for the tourists, it still retains plenty of charm, dignity and authenticity. This is mostly due to the premises themselves: a vast, dimly lit multilevel cellar.

⭐ PLAY

⭐ BURG KINO *Cinema*

☎ 587 84 06; www.burgkino.at; 01, Opernring 19; Ⓜ U1, U2, U4 Karlsplatz 🚊 D, 1, 2 🚌 59A, 62

The Burg Kino is a central cinema that shows only English-language films. It has regular screenings of the *The Third Man,* Carol Reed's timeless classic set in post-WWII Vienna, at 10.55pm Friday, 4.30pm Sunday and 4.55pm Tuesday.

⭐ BURGTHEATER *Theatre*

☎ 514 44 4140; www.burgtheater.at; 01, Dr-Karl-Lueger-Ring; tours adult/child €5.50/2, tickets €4-48; ⏱ box office 8am-6pm Mon-Fri, 9am-noon Sat & Sun; 🚊 D, 1, 2

The Burgtheater (National Theatre) is one of the prime theatre venues in the German-speaking world. Built in Renaissance style to designs by Gottfried Semper and Karl von Hasenauer, it had to be rebuilt after sustaining severe damage in WWII. The grand interior has stairway frescoes painted by the Klimt brothers, Gustav and Ernst.

⭐ HOFBURG CONCERT HALLS
Concert Venue

☎ 587 25 52; www.hofburgorchester.at; 01, Heldenplatz; tickets €39-52; U3 Herrengasse 🚊 D, 1, 2

The Neue Hofburg's concert halls, the sumptuous **Festsaal** and

VIENNA BOYS' CHOIR

As with Lipizzaner stallions and sausage stands, Vienna wouldn't be Vienna without the **Vienna Boys' Choir** (Wiener Sängerknaben; www.wsk.at). Founded more than five centuries ago by Maximilian I as the imperial choir, its members over the ages have included famed composers Schubert and Gallus, and conductors Richter and Krauss. Mozart composed for them in his day and Haydn was a member of another local choir but occasionally stepped in to sing with them. Today, it's the most famous boys' choir in the world, and consists of four separate choirs – hand selected each year and mainly Austrian – who share the demanding global tour schedule.

Catching the choir in concert takes some organisation. Tickets for their **Sunday performances** (☎ 533 99 27; www.bmbwk.gv.at, in German; ☾ 9.15am Oct-Jun) in the Hofburg's **Burgkapelle** (Royal Chapel; p38) should be booked around six weeks in advance. The choir also sings a mixed program of music in the **Musikverein** (below) at 4pm on Friday in May, June, September and October.

Redoutensaal, are regularly used for Strauss and Mozart concerts, featuring the Hofburg Orchestra and soloists from the Staatsoper and Volksoper.

⭐ JAZZLAND *Jazz Club*
☎ 533 25 75; www.jazzland.at, in German; 01, Franz-Josefs-Kai 29; ☾ 7.30pm-2am Mon-Sat Sep-Jun, from 7pm Mon-Sat Jul & Aug; Ⓜ U1, U4 Schwedenplatz Ⓣ 1, 2

Jazzland has been an institution of Vienna's jazz scene for more than 30 years. The music covers the whole jazz spectrum, from a grand mixture of local and international acts.

⭐ KURSALON *Concert Venue*
☎ 512 57 90; www.strauss-konzerte. at; 01, Johannesgasse 33; tickets €39-90; Ⓜ U4 Stadtpark, Ⓣ 1, 2

Fans of Strauss and Mozart will love the performances at Kursalon, which holds daily evening concerts (8.15pm) devoted to the two masters in a splendid, refurbished Renaissance building.

⭐ MUSIKVEREIN *Concert Venue*
☎ 505 81 90; www.musikverein.at; 01, Bösendorferstrasse 12; tours adult/child €5/3.50, tickets €4-90; ☾ box office 9am-8pm Mon-Fri, to 1pm Sat; Ⓜ U1, U2, U4 Karlsplatz Ⓣ D, 1, 2 Ⓑ 59A, 62

The Musikverein holds the proud title of the best acoustics of any concert hall in Austria, and the Vienna Philharmonic Orchestra makes excellent use of it. The interior is suitably lavish and can be visited on the occasional guided tour. Standing-room tickets in the main hall cost from €4 to €6; there are no student tickets.

⭐ PALAIS PALFFY *Club*

☎ 512 56 81; www.palais-palffy.at;
01, Josefsplatz 6; ⏱ 9pm-late Thu-Sat;
Ⓜ U3 Herrengasse

Two floors kick it up here – the first-floor lounge bar is topped by thousands of miniature glittering gemstones beneath a 12m chandelier with 80,000 Swarovski crystals. The luxurious upstairs dance floor is less glittery. Thursday is mixed electronic and pop, Friday features house, and the Jetlag Club (oldies, current dance) comes to town on Saturdays.

⭐ PASSAGE *Club*

☎ 961 88 00; www.sunshie.at; 01, Babenberger Passage, Burgring 1;
⏱ 8pm-4am Tue-Wed, 9pm-late Thu, 10pm-6am Fri & Sat; 🚊 D, 1, 2

Passage is the closest Vienna comes to a megaclub. Its sleek interior, soothing colours and sweaty atmosphere attract the beautiful people of the city, their entourages and plenty of oglers and barflies. Music is loud and fairly mainstream, with R'n'B, hip-hop and house nights; 'Disco Fever Tuesdays' draws some of the biggest crowds.

⭐ STAATSOPER *Concert Venue*

☎ 514 44 2250; www.wiener-staats oper.at; 01, Opernring 2; tours adult/child €5/2, incl Opera Museum Tue-Sun €6.50/3.50, tickets €2-54; ⏱ box office 9am to 1hr before performance Mon-Fri, to 5pm Sat; Ⓜ U1, U2, U4 Karlsplatz
🚊 D, 1, 2 🚌 59A, 62

The Staatsoper is *the* premier opera and classical-music venue in Vienna. Built between 1861 and 1869 by August Siccard von Siccardsburg and Eduard van der Nüll, it initially revolted the Viennese public and Habsburg royalty, quickly earning the nickname 'stone turtle'. Despite the frosty reception, its opening concert was Mozart's *Don Giovanni*. It went on to house some of the most iconic directors in history, including Gustav Mahler (who later moved on to New York's Metropolitan Opera House), Richard Strauss and Herbert von Karajan. In the interval, be sure to wander around the foyer and refreshment rooms to fully appreciate the gold and crystal interior.

⭐ VOLKSGARTEN *Club*

☎ 532 42 41; www.volksgarten.at, in German; 01, Burgring 1; Tue-Sat; Ⓜ U2, U3 Volkstheater 🚊 D, 1, 2, 49

Volksgarten serves a clientele eager to see and be seen. The long cocktail bar is perfect for people-watching and the music is an ever-rotating mix of hip-hop, house, salsa and reggae, but is hardly ever challenging. Opening hours are not fixed; dress upscale to glide past the bouncers.

MUSEUMSQUARTIER & NEUBAU

Some of the most vibrant areas of the Vorstädte (inner suburbs) congregate in Neubau (district 7). The culture-packed MQ, backing directly onto cobblestoned Spittelberg, anchors its western fringe, while a stroll around Zollergasse, Kirchengasse and Neubaugasse takes you into a lively district of idiosyncratic secondhand, alternative shops, and off-beat eating and drinking spots.

South of Neubau, across the busy but characterless Mariahilfer Strasse, you will find Mariahilf (district 6). Within this area, Gumpendorfer Strasse – once very run down – is enjoying a new lease on life, and is well-seeded with scruffy-chic restaurants and bars.

Together, these districts are lively and rich in cultural sights and great examples of Viennese everyday life – it's a part of town you might find yourself spending a lot of your time in.

MUSEUMSQUARTIER & NEUBAU

👁 SEE

🏠 SHOP

🍽 EAT

🍸 DRINK

⭐ PLAY

◉ SEE

◉ ARCHITEKTURZENTRUM WIEN

☎ 522 31 15; www.azw.at; 07, Museumsplatz 1; 1 exhibition adult/student €7/4.50, 2 exhibitions €9/6.50; ☉ 10am-7pm; ◉ U2 Museumsquartier, U2, U3 Volkstheater 🚋 49 🚌 2A, 48A

The Vienna Architecture Centre – comprising three halls used for temporary exhibitions, a library and a cafe – takes up much of the MQ north of MUMOK (right). Exhibitions focus on international architectural developments, and change on a regular basis.

◉ HOFMOBILIENDEPOT

☎ 524 33 570; www.hofmobiliendepot.at; 07, Andreasgasse 7; adult/under 19yr/concession/family €6.90/4.50/5.50/16; ☉ 10am-6pm Tue-Sun; ◉ U3 Zieglergasse

This is where furniture not displayed in the Hofburg, Schloss Schönbrunn, Belvedere Palace and other Habsburg residences is stored, along with a smattering of late-20th-century furniture. The collection is a highlight for anyone interested in furniture design and *Jugendstil* (art nouveau) furniture from the likes of Wagner, Loos and Hoffmann. In all, it's the most comprehensive collection of Biedermeier furniture in the world.

◉ KUNSTHALLE

☎ 521 89 33; www.kunsthallewien.at; 07, Museumsplatz 1; Hall 1 adult/under 13yr/concession €7.50/free/6, Hall 2 €6/free/4.50, combined ticket €10.50/free/8.50; ☉ 10am-7pm Fri-Wed, to 9pm Thu; ◉ U2 Museumsquartier, U3 Volkstheater 🚋 49 🚌 2A, 48A

Situated between the Leopold and MUMOK, the Kunsthalle (Art Hall) is a collection of exhibition

---

OTTO WAGNER BUILDINGS

Something of a problem zone due to flooding, the Wien River needed regulating in the late 19th century. More accurately, its last semblance of being a natural river was utterly and completely obliterated. At the same time, Otto Wagner had visions of turning the area between Karlsplatz and Schönbrunn into a magnificent boulevard. The vision blurred, and the reality is a gushing, concrete-bottomed creek (a shocking eyesore designed by Wagner) and a couple of attractive Wagner houses on the Linke Wienzeile. **Majolika-Haus** at No 40 (1899) is the prettiest as it's completely covered in glazed ceramic, with flowing floral motifs on the facade. The second of these *Jugendstil* (art nouveau) masterpieces is a corner house at **No 38**, which has reliefs from Kolo Moser and shapely bronze figures from Othmar Schimkowitz. Nearby, in **Köstlergasse 3**, is a third, simpler house and, finally, you can put Wagner's functionality to the test by descending into his **Kettenbrückengasse U-Bahn station**.

VIENNESE ACTIONISM

Viennese Actionism spanned the period from 1957 to 1968 and was one of the most extreme of all modern art movements. Its members experimented with surrealism and Dadaism in sound compositions and textual montages. The movement sought access to the unconscious through the frenzy of an extreme and very direct art. The Actionists quickly moved from pouring paint over a canvas or slashing it with knives to using politicised actions to address the sexual and social repression that pervaded the Austrian state. At one demonstration a man undressed, cut himself with a razor, urinated in a glass and drank his urine, smeared his body with faeces and sang the Austrian national anthem while masturbating.

halls used to showcase local and international contemporary art. Its high ceilings, open planning and functionality have helped the venue to leap-frog into the ranges of the top exhibition spaces in Europe. Programs rely heavily on photography, video, film, installations and new media.

☑ LEOPOLD MUSEUM

☎ 525 70-0; www.leopoldmuseum. org; 07, Museumsplatz 1; adult €10; ⏱ 10am-6pm Mon, Wed, Fri-Sun, to 9pm Thu; ⓔ U2 Museumsquartier, U2, U3 Volkstheater 🚌 2A, 48A

This museum is named after Rudolf Leopold, a Viennese ophthalmologist who amassed a huge private collection of mainly 19th-century and modernist Austrian artworks. Inside the white, limestone exterior is a 21m-high glass-covered atrium and plenty of open space. Rudolf Leopold loved Schiele, and the museum contains the largest collection of the painter's work in the world. The

collection does include drawings and graphics, but the originals are so sensitive to light that they are rarely exhibited.

☑ MUMOK

☎ 525 00-0; www.mumok.at; 07, Museumsplatz 1; adult/student & under 19yr/senior €9/free/7.20; ⏱ 10am-6pm Fri-Wed, to 9pm Thu; ⓔ U2 Museumsquartier, U2, U3 Volkstheater 🚌 49 🚌 2A, 48A

With a dark basalt edifice and sharp corners, the Museum Moderner Kunst houses Vienna's finest collection of 20th-century art, centred on fluxus, Nouveau Réalisme, pop art and Photorealism. The best of expressionism, cubism, minimal art and **Viennese Actionism** (see the boxed text, above) is represented in a collection of 9000 works that are rotated and exhibited by theme. Expect anything from photos of horribly deformed babies to naked bodies smeared with salad or an ultra–close-up of a urinating penis.

ZOOM

☎ 524 79 08; www.kindermuseum.
at, in German; 07, Museumsplatz 1;
🕑 8.30am-4pm Tue-Sun; Ⓜ U2 Museumsquartier, U2, U3 Volkstheater 🚌 2A
Zoom children's museum offers
arts and crafts sessions with a lot
of play thrown in. Children are
guided through themed programs
and have the chance to make,
break, draw, explore and, generally, be creative.

🏠 SHOP

BUCHHANDLUNG
WALTHER KÖNIG *Books*

☎ 512 85 88 0; 07, Museumsplatz 1;
🕑 10am-7pm Mon-Sat, from noon Sun;
Ⓜ U2, U3 Volkstheater 🚌 48A
A must for coffee-table-book con-
noisseurs, this lofty 250-sq-metre
space, with zinc shelves (to reflect
light) and baroque touches, hosts
a serious collection of books on
art, photography, fashion and
design theory, including a great

range on the history of Austrian
and Viennese art and design.

🏠 DAS MÖBEL
Furniture & Accessories

☎ 524 94 97; www.dasmoebel.at, in
German; 07, Burggasse 10; 🕑 10am-
1am; Ⓜ U2, U3 Volkstheater 🚌 48A
Das Möbel is more of a bar than a
shop (see p66), but it showcases
some of the funkiest and most
original furniture in Vienna. Local
artists and designers fill the place
with their latest creations, and
it's all for sale. The bags hanging
just inside the door, also locally
designed and produced, are truly
special creations.

🏠 HOLZER GALERIE
Furniture & Accessories, Jewellery

☎ 412 64 17; www.galerieholzer.at; 07,
Siebensterngasse 32; 🕑 10am-noon &
2-6pm Mon-Fri, 10am-5pm Sat; 🚌 49
This is the place for high-quality,
highly polished furniture, ornaments, lighting and art, mainly

---

SPITTELBERG

Directly behind the MuseumsQuartier (MQ) and bordered by Breitergasse, Siebenstren-
gasse, Sigmundgasse and Burggasse, this former red-light district became a highly coveted
slice of real estate decades ago, with less-than-quaint price tags. Today the area contains a
handful of shops, bars and restaurants (many overpriced), and its pedestrianised patchwork
of narrow cobblestoned streets and Biedermeier houses are stunning. Use the landscape
for pristine photo ops or, better yet, it's ideal for a romantic evening stroll. At Christmas, Spittelberg is transformed into one of the city's best-patronised **Christkindlmärkte**
(Christmas Markets; see p24), with craft stalls aplenty and city workers sipping *Glühwein*
(mulled wine).

Picture perfect at Lomoshop

KRZYSZTOF DYDYŃSKI

from the art deco and Bauhaus periods. If you simply must have that Josef Hoffman sideboard, shipping can be arranged. You'll also find some easier-to-transport art deco–inspired jewellery here.

🖿 LOMOSHOP *Photography*
☎ 523 70 16; 07, Museumsplatz 1; ☷ 11am-7pm Mon-Sun; ⊕ U2, U3 Volkstheater ☐ 48A

In MQ is the first ever Lomography shop of the **Lomographic Society** (www.lomography.com). Lomo is a worldwide cult and the Lomoshop is considered its heart. There's all manner of Lomo cameras,

gadgets and accessories for sale; an original Russian-made Lomo will set you back around €160, and you can get single-use disposable Lomo cameras for €14. There's also a wall full of Lomo photos on display, for inspiration.

🖿 MOT MOT *Clothing, Accessories*
☎ 924 27 19; www.motmotshop.com; 07, Kirchengasse 36; ☷ noon-7pm Tue-Fri, to 5pm Sat; ⊠ 49 ☐ 13A

This husband-and-wife team (both former graphic designers) create custom clothes with fun flair – each piece is screen printed by hand on American Apparel T-shirts and

Lucie Lamster-Thury

Former NYC stylist and owner of Shopping with Lucie (www.shopping withlucie.com), speciality shopping tours in Vienna.

What do you love most about shopping in Vienna? Most items are high quality and often have a personal touch – I also love that people are generally conscious consumers and concerned about sustainable living. **What's the best area of Vienna to wander if you want to stumble upon unusual boutiques?** Definitely Neubau. Each time I go, something new has opened up, and it's relaxing to wander around the atmospheric lanes. For example, on Saturdays you can barely move on busy Mariahilfer Strasse (where all the big-name shops are). But Lindengasse, which runs parallel to it one block away, is quiet and mellow, yet chock full of fascinating small shops. **Which shops do you recommend to visitors?** For made-on-the-premises clothes, head for The Hot Dogs (right) – the designer is often sewing right in the shop, and she churns out some of the most wearable clothes in the city at reasonable prices. If you're seeking something delicious made by small local producers, check out the confections, local wine and condiments at Austrian Delights (p46). All their items are manufactured here in Austria. And for a cross-section of the contemporary local design scene, Art Up (p46) is simply the best. It's a cooperative and carries anything from accessories to housewares to funky clothes.

sweatshirts; choose from more than 20 designs (imagine a comic book come to life) and colours. Their creations have caught the eye of a few celebrities: recent projects have included printing posters for The Kills and the Black Eyed Peas.

🏠 THE HOT DOGS *Fashion*

☎ 236 88 14; www.thehotdogs.org; 07, Zollergasse 12; ⏱ 1pm-7pm Tue-Fri, 11am-5pm Sat; 🚇 U3 Neubaugasse 🚌 13A

The Hot Dogs showcases individually tailored clothing for women; smooth lines and quality fabrics (raw silk, delicate wool, flowing-yet-structured cotton) dominate, yet most items sell for less than €200. Mandarina, designer and owner, is nearly always at the tiny table in the centre of the tiny space, sewing her latest creation.

🍴 EAT
🍴 DIE BURGERMACHER
Burgers   €

☎ 0699-11 58 95 99; 07, Burggasse 12; burgers €5.80-8.80; ⏱ 5.30-10pm Tue-Fri, 12.30-10pm Sat, closed Jul & Aug; 🚇 U2, U3 Volkstheater 🚋 46; ⊠ V

The interior of this small, alternative burger joint is simple, well styled and comfortable. The burgers here are made using organic ingredients and are served in meat and vegetarian varieties. If you

can't get a table, grab a spot at the side bench or get take away – in summer you can eat it in the MQ, just a few hops away.

🍴 GAUMENSPIEL
International, Beisl   €€

☎ 526 11 08; 07, Zieglergasse 54; mains €17.50-21.50, menu €32-40; ⏱ 6pm-midnight Mon-Sat; 🚋 49 🚌 48A; ⊠ V

Gaumenspiel is an immaculate, modern *Beisl* (small tavern) with a menu that changes every three weeks. The food is international, with a heavy Mediterranean influence, but you might also find braised veal cheeks with polenta, potato dumplings and artichokes. The decor is light in detail and the handful of streetside tables are popular in summer.

🍴 GLACIS BEISL *Neo-Beisl*   €€

☎ 526 56 60; 07, Museumsplatz; mains €8.90-17.60; ⏱ 11am-2am; 🚇 U2, U3 Volkstheater, U2 Museumsquartier; V

Hidden downstairs behind the buildings along Breitergasse (follow the signs from MUMOK) in the MQ, Glacis Beisl does an authentic *Gulasch* (goulash), an accomplished *Wiener Schnitzel* and some other very decent Austrian classics, which you can wash down with excellent Austrian reds and whites.

🍴 HALLE *International* €€

☎ 523 70 01; 07, Museumsplatz 1; mid-day menu €6.80-8.50, mains €6.90-16.50; 🕐 10am-2am; 🔵 U2 Museumsquartier, U2, U3 Volkstheater; 📶 Ⓥ

Halle is the versatile resident eatery of the Kunsthalle, with little kitchen downtime – the pots and pans are not hung up until midnight. The interior has plenty of optical tricks, such as cylindrical lamps and low tables, and the chefs churn out antipastos, pastas, salads, several Austrian all-rounders and pan-Asian dishes.

🍴 KANTINE *Cafe* €

☎ 523 82 39; 07, Museumsplatz 1; soups €2.90-5.90, wraps €5.10-6.40, light mains €7.20-8.90; 🕐 9am-2am Mon-Thu, to 4am Fri & Sat, to midnight Sun; 🔵 U2 Museumsquartier, U2, U3 Volkstheater; 📶 Ⓥ

This upbeat cafe-bar housed in the former stables of the emperor's personal steeds is the most laid-back spot to eat in the MQ. It has a couple of old sofas down the back where you can lounge about and surf in comfort, or you can grab a cocktail from the extensive list and make good use of the outdoor patio on MQ's main square.

🍴 RA'MIEN *Asian* €€

☎ 585 47 98; 06, Gumpendorfer Strasse 9; mains €7-16; 🕐 11am-midnight Tue-

Kantine, a laid-back cafe with a thoroughbred past

KRZYSZTOF DYDYNSKI

Sun, closed Aug; ◎ U2 Museumsquartier ⊟ 57A; Ⓥ

Picture a minimalist, grey-white room and lots of bright, young hip things bent over piping hot noodles – and you have Ra'mien. The menu covers a good swath of Asia, with a choice of Thai, Japanese, Chinese and Vietnamese noodle soups and rice dishes. Ra'mien fills up quickly at night, so it's best to book to avoid having to wait for a table; the lounge-bar downstairs has regular DJs and stays open until at least 2am.

🍴 SCHON SCHÖN
International   €€

☎ 0699-153 777 01; 07, Lindengasse 53; 3–6-course menu €36-46; ◔ 11am-11pm Tue-Sat; ◎ U3 Zieglergasse

Dining is a unique social experience at this eatery in Neubau. With only one table (seating about 20), you'll certainly get to know your immediate fellow diners, if not the whole table. The imaginative cuisine changes daily, but always includes a handful of vegetarian and meat or fish dishes. It's gay-run but attracts both genders; a groovy lounge area downstairs is open from 7pm to 2am Thursday to Saturday.

🍴 ZU DEN 2 LIESERLN *Beisl*   €

☎ 523 32 82; 07, Burggasse 63; lunch menu €4.90-5.30, mains €6-11.90; ◔ 11am-11pm; ⊟ 48A

A classic budget *Beisl* of legendary status, Zu den 2 Lieserln has been serving celebrities, politicians, office workers and students for decades. Six varieties of schnitzel crowd the menu (the *Haus Schnitzel,* filled with gorgonzola, ham and pepperoni, is killer bee) alongside other Viennese options. The wood panelling, simple wooden chairs and chequered tablecloths create a quaint and cosy interior, complemented by a tree-shaded inner courtyard.

🍸 DRINK
🍸 CAFÉ DRECHSLER
Coffee House

☎ 587 85 80; 06, Linke Wienzeile 22; ◔ 8am-2am Mon, 3am-2am Tue-Sat, 3am-midnight Sun; ◎ U4 Kettenbrückengasse

One of the liveliest coffee houses in town, Drechsler re-opened with a smash after extensive renovations (Sir Terence Conran worked his magic with polished marble bar and table tops, Bauhaus light fixtures and whitewashed timber panels – stylish yet still distinctly Viennese). Besides the usual coffee-house suspects, its *Gulasch* (served 23 hours a day) is legendary, as are the tunes the DJ spins, which always keep the vibe upbeat and hip.

▼ CAFÉ LEOPOLD *Bar, Cafe*

☎ 523 67 32; 07, Museumsplatz 1;
🕑 9am-2am Sun-Wed, to 4am Thu-Sat;
Ⓜ U2 Museumsquartier; 🛜

The pick of the MQ bars, Café Leopold sits high at the top of the Leopold Museum (p59). Its design is sleek and smart, its conservatory overlooks the MQ's square and the atmosphere is more club than bar (DJs feature Monday to Saturday).

▼ CAFÉ SPERL *Cafe*

☎ 586 41 58; 06, Gumpendorfer Strasse 11; 🕑 7am-11pm Mon-Sat, 11am-8pm Sun (closed Sun in summer); 🚌 57A; 🛜

With its gorgeous *Jugendstil* fittings, grand dimensions, cosy booths and unhurried air, Sperl is one of the finest coffee houses in Vienna. And that's to say nothing of a menu that features *Sperl Torte* – a mouth-watering mix of almonds and chocolate cream. Grab a slice and a newspaper, order a strong coffee, and join the rest of the patrons people-watching and day-dreaming.

▼ DAS MÖBEL *Bar, Cafe*

☎ 524 94 97; 07, Burggasse 10;
🕑 10am-1am; Ⓜ U2, U3 Volkstheater
🚌 48A; 🛜

Das Möbel wins points for its furniture, consisting entirely of one-off pieces produced by local designers. Half the fun is choosing a spot

Swap art-browsing for people-watching at Café Leopold

KRZYSZTOF DYDYNSKI

that takes your fancy – whether it be in a swinging chair or on a surfboard bench. Light fittings, bags and various odds and ends complete the look, and everything is for sale.

EBERT'S COCKTAIL BAR
Cocktail Bar

☎ 586 54 65; 06, Gumpendorfer Strasse 101; ⏰ 6pm-2am Sun-Thu, 7pm-4am Fri & Sat; ◉ U3 Neubaugasse

Expert bartenders shake it up: all the mixologists here double as instructors at the bartending academy next door. The cocktail list reads like a novel, the vibe is stylish modern minimalism, the tunes are jazzy to electronic and on weekends you'll barely squeeze in.

ELEKTRO GÖNNER *Bar*

☎ 208 66 79; 06, Mariahilfer Strasse 101; ⏰ 7pm-2am Sun-Thu, to 4am Fri & Sat; ◉ U3 Zieglergasse

Elektro Gönner is an unpretentious bar opened by architects (and attracting plenty from the profession). Much of the interior is uncomplicated and bare, aside from the occasional art installation in the back room, and the music is diverse. The bar hides at the back of a courtyard off Mariahilfer Strasse.

EUROPA *Bar, Cafe*

☎ 526 33 83; 07, Zollergasse 8; ⏰ 9am-5am; ◉ U3 Neubaugasse 🚌 13A; 🛜

A long-standing fixture of the 7th district, Europa is a chilled spot any time of day or night. During the sunny hours, join the relaxed set at a window table for coffee and food, and in the evening take a pew at the bar and enjoy the DJ's tunes. Breakfast, served between 9am and 3pm daily, caters to a hung-over clientele; Sunday features a sumptuous breakfast buffet (€9.50).

FUTUREGARDEN BAR & ART CLUB *Bar, Club*

☎ 585 26 13; 06, Schadekgasse 6; ⏰ 6pm-2am Mon-Sat, from 8pm Sun; ◉ U3 Neubaugasse 🚌 13A

With white walls, an open bar and basic furniture, it's hard to find a simpler place in Vienna. Its one piece of decoration – apart from the occasional art exhibition by local artists – is its rectangular disco 'ball', which swings from the ceiling. Futuregarden attracts a late 20s and 30s crowd with its cool atmosphere and electric sounds.

JOANELLI *Bar, Wine Bar*

☎ 311 84 04; 06, Gumpendorfer Strasse 47; ⏰ 6pm-2am; ◉ U3 Neubaugasse

Vienna's oldest *Eissalon* (ice-cream shop; the ancient sign still hangs above the entrance) has morphed into an arty hang-out, with colourful lighting (sometimes pink, sometimes yellow) casting shadows on the plain white formica tables and empty walls. In addition to relaxed tunes, the drinks list contains more than 20 quality wines by the glass (most of them Austrian) – the staff expertly guides you between the *Blauburgunders* and the *Veltiners*. A full cocktail and beer menu, plus nibbles, is on offer, too.

▼ **LUTZ** *Bar, Club*
☎ 585 36 46; 06, Mariahilfer Strasse 3; ☽ from 8am Mon-Fri, from 9am Sat, from 10am Sun; ☺ U3 Neubaugasse ➁ 13A; ⌂

Although it's open during the day as a cafe and restaurant, evening is when to hit this modern, open space. A bar for everyone, it boasts a fab location in the heart of the shopping district – try to snag a seat at the floor-to-ceiling windows gazing down on busy Mariahilfer Strasse. On weekends, a subterranean club opens from 9.30pm, playing anything from house to disco.

▼ **MANGO BAR** *Gay Bar*
☎ 587 44 48; 06, Laimgrubengasse 3; ☽ 9pm-4am; ☺ U4 Kettenbrücken-gasse ➁ 57A

Mango attracts a young, often men-only gay crowd with good music, friendly staff and plenty of mirrors to check out yourself and others. It usually serves as a kick-start for a big night out on the town.

▼ **MON AMI** *Bar*
☎ 585 01 34; 06, Theobaldgasse 9; ☽ 4pm-1am Mon-Sat; ☺ U4 Neubaugasse

Don't let the dog-and-cat-grooming sign fool ya: this former pet-grooming salon has morphed into a lovely '60s-style bar that mixes excellent cocktails; serves a short but decent beer, wine and snacks list; and attracts a laid-back and unpretentious crowd. The rear of the bar is a shop (open to 10pm) stocking creations by young designers, so you can pick up a groovy new top and kick a few back in less than 10 steps.

▼ **PHIL** *Bar, Cafe*
☎ 581 04 89; 06, Gumpendorfer Strasse 10-12; ☽ 9am-1am Tue-Sun, from 5pm Mon; ➁ 57A

A retro bar reminiscent of an East Berlin *Lokal*, Phil attracts a bohemian crowd happy to squat on kitsch furniture like your grandmother used to own. Half the establishment is store rather than bar; TVs from the '70s, DVDs, records and books are for sale, as is all the furniture. The staff is super-friendly and the vibe as relaxed as can be.

▼ **SIEBENSTERNBRÄU**
Microbrewery
☎ 523 86 97; www.7stern.at; 07, Siebensterngasse 19; ☽ 10am-midnight; ➁ 49

This microbrewery features all the main varieties of beer, plus hemp, chilli and smoky (the malt is dried over an open fire); the hidden back garden is sublime in the warmer months.

☙ TANZCAFÉ JENSEITS *Bar, Club*
☎ 587 12 33; 06, Nelkengasse 3;
🕑 9pm-4am Mon-Sat; ☺ U3 Neubaugasse 🚌 13A

The red-velvet interior that might be out of a '70s bordello is a soothing backdrop for a night out at Jenseits. The tiny dance floor fills to overflowing on Fridays and Saturdays, with relaxed revellers slowly moving around each other to soul and funk.

☙ TOP KINO BAR *Bar*
☎ 208 30 00; 06, Rahlgasse 1; 🕑 10am-2am; ☺ U2 Museumsquartier 🚌 57A

Occupying the foyer of the cinema Top Kino, this bar is a pleasantly relaxed place that attracts a fashionable alternative crowd. The decor is highly retro, and there are tunes to match the furniture. Kozel, one of the Czech Republic's better Pilsners, is lined up against Austria's finest lagers.

☙ WIRR *Bar*
☎ 929 40 50; www.wirr.at, in German; 07, Burggasse 70; 🕑 11am-2am Mon-Wed, to 4am Thu & Fri, 10am-late Sat & Sun; 🚌 48A

On weekends it's often hard to find a seat – particularly on the comfy sofas – at this colourful, alternative bar. Its rooms are spacious and open, the walls are covered in local artists' work, including a large (albeit bizarre) tie collection, and light snacks are available. Eclectic clubbing – ranging from '60s pop to Balkan rhythms – is well attended in the downstairs club.

☆ PLAY

☆ AUX GAZELLES *Club*
☎ 585 66 45; www.auxgazelles.at; 06, Rahlgasse 5; 🕑 11pm-4am Thu-Sat; ☺ U2 Museumsquartier 🚌 57A

Aux Gazelles' club-bar is beautifully Moorish and suitably filled with beautiful people. The music is an eclectic mix of smooth ethnic sounds, and there are plenty of dim corners and low, comfy couches to escape to if so desired. The rest of this gigantic club venue features a restaurant, bar and deli, and there's even a *hammam* (steam bath). Aux Gazelles is one of the few clubs in town where a dress code is enforced.

☆ ROTE BAR *Live Music Venue, Bar*
☎ 521 11 2 18; www.rotebar.at; 07, Neustiftgasse 1; 🕑 10pm-late; ☺ U2, U3 Volkstheater 🚋 D, 1, 2, 49

This marble-, chandelier- and red-velvet-curtain-bedecked

NEIGHBOURHOODS

MUSEUMSQUARTIER & NEUBAU

Enjoy the theatre of drinking at Rote Bar (p69)

KRZYSZTOF DYDYNSKI

space in the nether regions of the Volkstheater hosts Tuesday night jazz sessions, Saturday dance nights with DJs, Wednesday readings and performance art, plus occasional one-offs such as Milonga nights – where you can try to Tango.

⭐ TANZQUARTIER WIEN
Dance Venue
☎ 581 35 91; www.tqw.at; 07, Museumsplatz 1; tickets €11-18; ⏰ box office 1hr before performances; ⓜ U2 Museumsquartier, U2, U3 Volkstheater 🚌 2A
Tanzquartier Wien, located in the MQ, is Vienna's first dance institution. It hosts an array of

local and international performances with a strong experimental nature. Students receive advance tickets at 30% of the price, or €7, for unsold seats 15 minutes before show time.

⭐ VOLKSTHEATER *Theatre*
☎ 523 05 89 77; www.volkstheater.at, in German; 07, Neustiftgasse 1; tickets €8-45; ⏰ box office 10am-performance Mon-Sat Sep-Jun, reduced hrs late Jun-Aug; ⓜ U2, U3 Volkstheater 🚌 D, 1, 2, 49
With a seating capacity close to 1000, the Volkstheater is one of Vienna's largest theatres. Built in 1889, its interior is suitably

grand. While most performances are translations (anything from Woody Allen to Ingmar Bergman or Molière), only German-language shows are produced.

Students can buy unsold tickets one hour before performances start for €3.60. Be sure to grab a drink before or after the show at the Rote Bar (p69).

JOSEFSTADT & ALSERGRUND

Josefstadt and Alsergrund form the northwest and northern borders of the suburbs flanking the Innere Stadt. While Josefstadt is short on sights, it offers a healthy sprinkling of eating and drinking spots. Alsergrund, with its Liechtenstein and Sigmund Freud museums, contains sights and eating spots in abundance.

Most of the area is upmarket, but to the west lies the Gürtel (which literally means belt, but refers to a large ring road encompassing the inner suburbs). This section is a tad grittier, and is filled with a slew of exceptional bars and clubs housed in the *Stadtbogen* (spaces beneath the arches of the elevated subway line). The closer you move towards the Ringstrasse and the Innere Stadt, the more the architecture takes on a Biedermeier flavour.

Alsergrund is also home to a large university, which equals oodles of bars and cheap restaurants packed with student life, and the unusual Fernwärme – a waste incinerator transformed into a colourful landmark by Friedensreich Hundertwasser.

JOSEFSTADT & ALSERGRUND

NEIGHBOURHOODS

JOSEFSTADT & ALSERGRUND

👁 SEE

👁 BEETHOVEN WOHNUNG HEILIGENSTADT

☎ 370 54 08; 19, Probusgasse 6; adult/under 19yr €2/free; ⏰ 10am-1pm & 2-6pm Tue-Sun; 🚃 D 🚌 38A

When one of the world's greatest composers turned stone deaf, he sought a cure from Heiligenstadt's mineral waters. The musical wonder wrote his second symphony in this apartment.

👁 FERNWÄRME

☎ 313 26-0; 09, Spittelauer Lände 45; admission free; 🚇 U4, U6 Spittelau 🚃 D

The exterior of Friedensreich Hundertwasser's wonderfully pimped rubbish dump is a visual bonanza of colours topped by a glistening chimney stack that culminates in an Arab-esque golden bulb. Free exhibitions by or about local artists take place in the foyer, and each summer open-air concerts are held in the yard – including some in conjunction with Jazz Fest Wien.

👁 LIECHTENSTEIN MUSEUM

☎ 319 57 670, concert bookings 319 57 67-252; www.liechtensteinmuseum.at; 09, Fürstengasse 1; adult/under 16yr €10/free; ⏰ 10am-5pm Fri-Tue; 🚃 D 🚌 40A

The royal family of Liechtenstein resided in Vienna until the An-

STRUDELHOFSTIEGE

The Strudelhofstiege is a *Jugendstil* (art nouveau) staircase from 1910 that forms a winding cascade of steps into Liechtensteinstrasse, with two fountains integrated into it. At night it is lit up gloriously. It's named after Peter von Strudel, who took Vienna into the high baroque period in the late 16th and early 17th century.

schluss (the annexation of Austria by Germany in 1938). Prince Hans-Adam II's private collection (200 paintings and 50 sculptures dating from 1500 to 1700) is now on display in this palace. Don't miss the **Herkulessaal** (Hercules Hall) – so named for the Hercules motifs within its ceiling frescoes by renowned Roman painter Andrea Pozzo (1642–1709).

👁 SCHUBERT GEBURTSHAUS

☎ 317 36 01; 09, Nussdorfer Strasse 54; adult/under 19yr €2/free; ⏰ 10am-1pm & 2-6pm Tue-Sun; 🚃 37, 38

Young Franz was born in the kitchen here, and apart from his trademark glasses, the house is rather short on objects. But 'Schubertologists' like to trek here, especially to catch the occasional concert. Bizarrely, a couple of rooms of the house are given over to Adalbert Stifter (1805–68) and his Biedermeier paintings.

One person's trash, another person's treasure – the Fernwärme

KRZYSZTOF DYDYNSKI

SERVITENKIRCHE

☎ 317 61 95-0; www.rossau.at, in German; 09, Servitengasse 9; Ⓞ U4 Rossauer Lände 🚋 D

Dominating the Serviten Quarter – a small confluence of cobblestone streets lined with bars, restaurants and shops – is the Servitenkirche, the only church outside the Innere Stadt to survive the second Turkish siege of 1683. It's only open for Mass, but you can peer through the iron railings at the baroque interior and oval nave.

SIGMUND FREUD MUSEUM

☎ 319 15 96; www.freud-museum.at; 09, Berggasse 19; adult/child €7/4.50; ⏱ 9am-6pm Jul-Sep, to 5pm Oct-Jun; 🚋 D

The apartment where the father of psychoanalysis lived and worked from 1891 until his forced departure from Vienna with the arrival of the Nazis in 1938 is now a museum. It contains a number of his possessions, and his obsessions – travelling, smoking and collecting ancient art – are well represented; there are Egyptian and Buddhist statues everywhere.

VOTIVKIRCHE

09, Rooseveltplatz; ⏱ 9am-1pm & 4-6pm Tue-Sat, 9am-1pm Sun; Ⓞ U2 Schottentor 🚋 37, 38, 40-44

In 1853 Franz Josef I survived an assassination attempt when a knife-wielding Hungarian failed to

The neoclassicist library adds spine to the Liechtenstein Museum (p74)

KRZYSZTOF DYDYNSKI

find the emperor's neck through his collar. The twin-towered neo-Gothic Votive Church was commissioned in thanks for his lucky escape. Frescoes and bulbous chandeliers enliven the rather bleak interior, but the prize exhibit is the 1460 Antwerp Altar in the **church museum** (☎ 406 11 92; adult €3.90; ☽ 4-6pm Mon-Fri, 10am-1pm Sat).

⦀ EAT

⦀ GASTHAUS WICKERL *Beisl* €€
☎ 317 74 89; 09, Porzellangasse 24a; midday menu €6.20, mains €7.90-16; ☽ 9am-midnight Mon-Fri, 10am-midnight Sat, 10am-4pm Sun; ▣ D

Wickerl is a lovely *Beisl* with an all-wood finish and a warm, welcoming mood. Seasonal fare – such as *Kürbiscremesuppe* (cream of pumpkin soup) and *Kürbisgulasch* (pumpkin goulash) in autumn, *Marillenknödel* (apricot dumplings) in summer and *Spargel* (asparagus) in spring – are mixed with the usual Viennese offerings of *Tafelspitz* (prime boiled beef), *Zwiebelrostbraten* (slices of roast beef smothered in gravy and fried onions), and veal and pork schnitzel.

⦀ STOMACH *Austrian* €€
☎ 310 20 99; 09, Seegasse 26; mains €10-18; ☽ 4pm-midnight Wed-Sat, 10am-10pm Sun; ⦿ U4 Rossauer Lände

Stomach's menu brims with meat and vegetarian delights, such as Styrian roast beef, cream of pumpkin soup and, when in season, wild boar and venison. The interior is authentically rural-Austrian, and the overgrown garden creates a picturesque backdrop. The name comes from the rearrangement of the word Tomaschek, the butcher's shop originally located here. Reservations are highly recommended.

🍴 SUPPENWIRTSCHAFT
Soups & Salads   €
☎ 317 67 45; 09, Servitengasse 6; soups €4.50-5.80; 🕙 11.30am-6pm Mon-Fri; 🚇 D; ✗ Ⓥ

This chic little eat-in and take-away kitchen focuses mainly on soups and a few curries and salads from a weekly menu. Russian *Borscht* (beetroot soup) may be served alongside pear soup one week, and all are made fresh each day using ingredients sourced at the Naschmarkt.

🍴 WEINKELLEREI ENRICO PANIGL *Italian*   €€
☎ 406 52 18; 08, Josefstädter Strasse 91; mains €19-25; 🕙 6pm-1am; 🚇 U6 Josefstädter Strasse 🚋 2 🚌 13A

This wine restaurant (the menu offers more than 150 wines from Italy and Austria) serves delicious

---

WORTH THE TRIP
One block west of Josefstadt, Ottakring, the 16th district, is home to the **Brunnenmarkt** (16, Brunnengasse; 🕙 6am-6.30pm Mon-Fri, to 2pm Sat; 🚇 U6 Josefstädter Strasse 🚋 2, 44). Named after the street it takes over, this is the largest street market in Vienna and worth a visit to absorb the neighbourhood's ethnic make-up – most stallholders are of Turkish or Balkan descent. The majority of produce sold (all at rock-bottom prices) is vegetables and fruit, but you'll also encounter a few stalls selling tacky clothes (Hulk Hogan T-shirt, anyone?). It's a fantastic place for a satisfying bargain meal – the kebab houses are superb; one of the best is neighbourhood fave **Kent** (☎ 405 91 73; 16, Brunnengasse 67; mains €5-10; 🕙 6am-2am; 🚇 U6 Josefstädterstrasse 🚋 J).

At the northern end of the market, **Yppenplatz** is a tranquil square with a smattering of hip cafes and restaurants, and one standout shop, **Stauds** (☎ 406 88 05-21; http://stauds.com; 16, Yppenplatz; 🕙 8am-12.30pm Tue-Thu & Sat, 8am-12.30pm & 3.30-6pm Fri; 🚇 U6 Josefstädter Strasse 🚋 2, 44). This family business has been making jams and pickled vegetables and fruit for more than 30 years and the quality is by far the best in Vienna. On Saturday, the square is also home to the best *Bauernmarkt* (farmers market) in the city, where growers from the surrounding countryside come to sell their wares.

Erich Wassicek
Owner of Halbestadt (right)

What defines the Viennese bar scene? Well, people don't just drink at bars, people often spend an evening just having beers and enjoying quiet conversation at a *Kaffeehaus* (coffee house). **What areas should visitors explore to experience the local scene?** Wieden (p84), especially Schleifmühlegasse and Margaretenstrasse, is great if you want hip and slightly bohemian bars that buzz most evenings. There's also a cool selection of quirky bars on and around Gumpendorferstrasse in Mariahilf (p56). **What do you love best about Vienna?** It's such a low-stress city, so phlegmatic. Plus it is a small city with world-class cultural offerings – essentially, you get the best of both worlds. **On your evening off, where do you go for a drink?** Kruger's American Bar (p52), for quality cocktails in a traditional setting.

dishes such as tuna with truffle and porcini sauce accompanied by grilled polenta (€19.90). The atmosphere is genuinely rustic, right down to the wooden floors, offset by art from Vienna's postmodernist guru Hermann Nitsch.

☗ DRINK

☗ CAFÉ BERG *Gay Bar*
☎ 319 57 20; 09, Berggasse 8; ☽ 10am-1am Oct-Jun, to midnight Jul-Sep; ◉ U2 Schottentor ☒ 37, 38, 40, 41, 42, 43, 44 ☒ 40A; 📶

Café Berg is Vienna's leading gay bar, although it's welcoming to all walks of life. Its staff are some of the nicest in town, the layout sleek and smart and the vibe chilled. Its bookshop, **Löwenherz** (☽ 10am-7pm Mon-Fri, to 5pm Sat), stocks a grand collection of gay magazines and books.

☗ CAFÉ HUMMEL *Coffee House*
☎ 405 53 14; 08, Josefstädter Strasse 66; ☽ 7am-midnight Mon-Sat, from 8am Sun; ☒ 5, 33; 📶

Unpretentious and classic, Hummel is a large *Kaffeehaus* catering to a regular Josefstadt crowd. The coffee is rich, the cakes baked on the premises and the waiters typically snobbish. In summer, it's easy to spend a few hours in Hummel's outdoor seating area, mulling over the international papers and watching the human traffic on Josefstädter Strasse.

☗ CHELSEA *Bar, Club*
☎ 407 93 09; www.chelsea.co.at, in German; 08, Lerchenfelder Gürtel 29-31; ☽ 6pm-4am Mon-Sat, from 4pm Sun; ◉ U6 Thaliastrasse ☒ 46

Chelsea is the old, ratty dog on the Gürtel and very much a favourite of the student and alternative scenes. Posters and underground paraphernalia adorn walls and DJs spin loud sounds (usually indie, sometimes techno) when live acts aren't playing.

☗ FRAUENCAFÉ *Gay Bar*
☎ 406 37 54; 08, Lange Gasse 8; ☽ 6pm-midnight Thu & Fri; ☒ 46

A strictly women-only, lesbian and transgender cafe-bar, Frauencafé has long been a favourite of Vienna's lesbian scene. It has a homely, relaxed feel and is located away from the hub of gay and lesbian bars around the Rosa Lila Villa.

☗ HALBESTADT *Cocktail Bar*
☎ 319 47 35; 09, Stadtbogen 155; ☽ 6pm-2am Mon-Thu, 7pm-4am Fri & Sat, closed Sun; ◉ U6 Nussdorferstrasse

It starts when you can't open the glass door. The host swings it forth, escorts you in, takes your coat and offers to advise you on what to order – impeccable hospitality, no snobbery. More than 500 bottles grace the walls of the tiny space under the *Bogen* (subway arches) and mixologists hold court creating tongue-enticing works of art, which are shaken and poured into exquisite receptacles: South Pacific–inspired drinks arrive in ceramic goblets and *Sekt* (sparkling wine) in retro champagne glasses. See the interview on p78 for more.

▼ HIRT *Heuriger*
☎ 318 96 41; 19, Eisernhandgasse 165, Kahlenberg; ◷ 2pm-late Wed-Sat; ▣ 38A

Hidden among the vineyards on the eastern slopes of Kahlenberg, Hirt is a simple *Heuriger* (wine tavern) with few frills. Basic wooden tables, a small buffet and marginal service all help to create a traditional atmosphere. Views of Kahlenbergerdorf and the 21st district across the Danube are a pleasure to enjoy over a few glasses of wine in the early evening. Also open from 10am Sunday in every odd month and the first half of December.

▼ MAYER AM PFARRPLATZ
Heuriger
☎ 370 12 87; 19, Pfarrplatz 2, Nussdorf; ◷ 4pm-midnight Mon-Sat, from 11am Sun; ▣ 38A

Fifteen minutes' walk from U4 Heiligenstadt U-Bahn station, Mayer caters to tour groups but still manages to retain an air of authenticity, helped along by its peaceful

ambience, vine-covered surrounds and history (Beethoven lived here in 1817). The huge shaded garden towards the rear includes a children's play area, and there's live music from 7pm to 11pm daily.

▼ REINPRECHT *Heuriger*
☎ 320 14 71; 19, Cobenzlgasse 22, Grinzing; ◷ 3.30pm-midnight mid-Feb–mid-Dec; ▣ 38A

Located in a former monastery in the heart of Grinzing, Reinprecht shines bright among the otherwise dull *Heurigen* in these parts. It still caters to the masses with its huge garden, enormous buffet and live music, but quality reigns throughout. It has won numerous awards over the years and features some of the best wine in the city. Check out the cork collection; at 3500 pieces, it's the largest in Europe.

▼ RHIZ *Bar, Club*
☎ 409 25 05; 08, Lerchenfelder Gürtel 37-38; ◷ 6pm-4am Mon-Sat, to 2am Sun; ◉ U6 Josefstädter Strasse ▣ 2, 33; 🛜

Rhiz's decor of brick arches and glass walls is reminiscent of so many bars beneath the U6 line, but its status as a stalwart of the city's electronica scene gives it the edge over much of the competition. Black-clad boozers and an alternative set cram the interior to

A window on Vienna at Weinstube Josefstadt

KRZYSZTOF DYDYNSKI

hear DJs and live acts, while the large outdoor seating area fills to overflowing.

☿ SHIRAZ Cocktail Bar, Hookah Bar
☎ 335 55 55; 09, Stadtbogen 185; ⏱ 6pm–2am; ⊖ U6 Nussdorferstrasse
Step into *1001 Nights* at this *shisha* bar-club-cocktail bar. Puff on hookahs, lounge in plush sofas and contemplate the oriental red-and-gold wallpaper butting up against brick arches. Exotic mixed drinks and a long list of (mainly Austrian and new world) wines lubricate while DJs spin international tunes and bodies boogie into the starry night.

☿ WEIN & WASSER Wine Bar
☎ 403 53 45; 08, Laudongasse 57; ⏱ 6pm–1am Mon-Sat; ⊖ U6 Josefstrasse ⊞ 5
Wine & Water is the best place in Vienna to sample Austrian wine outside a *Heuriger* – more than 20 Austrian wines are served by the glass. Kick back in the subterranean space with arched bricks flanked by pale-yellow lighting and flickering candles. Nibbles and tapas round out the menu.

☿ WEINSTUBE JOSEFSTADT
Stadtheuriger
☎ 406 46 28; 08, Piaristengasse 27; ⏱ 4pm–midnight Apr-Dec; ⊞ 2 ⊟ 13A
Weinstube Josefstadt is one the loveliest *Stadtheurigen* in the city.

SNOW GLOBES

There are many impersonators but only one true snow-globe original – the Perzy Snow Globe. Back in 1900 in his workshop in Vienna, Erwin Perzy I had the idea of designing a globe containing a church and filled with liquid and rice, which, when shaken, produced the effect of snow falling. It became an instant hit, even with Emperor Franz Josef.

These days Erwin Perzy III, the grandson of the snow-globe creator, runs the company. These snow globes have landed in some illustrious paws – a Perzy snow globe was produced for Bill Clinton's inauguration and contains the actual confetti from the event. One-off pieces have also been produced for the films *Citizen Kane*, *Heidi* and *True Lies*.

In a world of cheap-and-cheerful products, churned out in their thousands by automated production lines, it's refreshing that Perzy snow globes are still handmade. The factory (tours by appointment only) contains a **Perzy Snow Globe Museum** (☎ 486 43 41; www .viennasnowglobe.at; 17, Schumanngasse 87; ☉ 9am-3pm Mon-Thu; ⓑ 9, 42).

Its garden is a barely controlled green oasis among concrete residential blocks, and tables are squeezed in between the trees and shrubs. Food is typical, with a buffet-style selection and plenty of cheap meats (chicken wings go for only €1). The friendly, well-liquored locals come free of charge. The location is not well signposted; the only sign of its existence is a metal *Busch'n* (green wreath or branch) hanging from a doorway.

⭐ PLAY

⭐ CAFÉ CARINA *Live Music Venue*
☎ 406 43 22; www.café-carina.at, in German; 08, Josefstädter Strasse 84; ☉ 6pm-2am Mon-Thu, to 4am Fri & Sat; ⓤ U6 Josefstädter Strasse ⓑ 2, 33
Small, smoky and pleasantly dingy, Carina is a muso's and drinker's bar. Local bands perform most nights,

only a few feet from a normally enthusiastic audience. The music is invariably folk, jazz or country.

⭐ INTERNATIONAL THEATRE *Theatre*
☎ 319 62 72; www.international theatre.at; 09, Porzellangasse 8; tickets €20-25; ☉ box office 11am-3pm Mon-Fri, plus 6pm-7.30pm on performance days; ⓑ D
The small International Theatre, with its entrance on Müllnergasse, has a mainly American company who live locally. Discounted tickets are available to students and senior citizens (€15). It closes around early-July through to mid-September.

⭐ VIENNA'S ENGLISH THEATRE *Theatre*
☎ 402 12 60-0; www.englishtheatre. at; 08, Josefsgasse 12; tickets €22-42;

KRZYSZTOF DYDYNSKI

Where English is spoken and the speare is shaken

⏱ box office 10am-7.30pm Mon-Fri, 5pm-7.30pm Sat (when performances are scheduled); Ⓜ U2 Rathaus 🚋 2 🚌 13A
Founded in 1963, Vienna's English Theatre is the oldest foreign-language theatre in Vienna (it also has an occasional show in French or Italian). Productions range from timeless pieces such as Shakespeare through to contemporary works. Students receive 20% discount on all tickets; standby tickets for €9 go on sale 15 minutes before show time.

⭐ WIENER RESIDENZORCHESTER
Concert Venue
☎ 817 21 78; www.wro.at; 08, Auerspergstrasse 1; tickets €39-54; ⏱ 8.15pm daily Mar-early Jan; Ⓜ U2, U3 Volkstheater 🚋 D, 1, 2, 49
The Vienna Residence Orchestra's philosophy and mission is to present Viennese classics in their full glory and purest form. It specialises in Wolfgang Amadeus Mozart and Johann Strauss. Concerts are held at the opulent Auersperg palace, where musicians showcase their talents while dressed head-to-toe in rococo and Biedermeier costumes. There is no box office – call or order tickets online.

WIEDEN & AROUND

Bohemian Wieden (district 4) and its surrounds is light on sights, but contains one of the capital's most exciting and rapidly gentrifying areas. At Wieden's northeast corner sits the Karlskirche, one of the city's finest baroque churches. Further south lies Kettenbrückengasse, the division between Wieden and neighbouring Margareten (district 5). This borderland between the two districts boasts the most alternative feel. In and around the junction of Schleifmühlgasse and Margaretenstrasse is a high concentration of bars and clubs that places this area high on the list of destinations for a good night out. Lining the northwestern edges of the area is the Wien River and a strip of concrete sandwiched between the Rechte and Linke Wienzieles, covering where the river used to flow. This is where the Naschmarkt takes over. The market is an energetic blend of restaurants, shops and low-key ethnic stalls, begging you to eat and stroll, stroll and eat, over and over again.

WIEDEN & AROUND

◉ SEE

◉ KARLSKIRCHE

☎ 712 44 56; www.karlskirche.at, in German; 04, Karlsplatz; adult/under 10yr €6/free; ⏱ 9am-noon & 1-6pm Mon-Sat, 1-5.30pm Sun; ◉ U1, U2, U4 Karlsplatz

Karlskirche rises up at the south-east corner of Resselpark and is the finest of Vienna's baroque churches. Enormous twin columns at the front are modelled on Trajan's Column in Rome and show scenes from the life of St Charles Borromeo (who helped plague victims in Italy), to whom the church is dedicated.

◉ NASCHMARKT

06, Linke Wienzeile/Rechte Wienzeile; ◉ U4 Kettenbrückengasse

Of Vienna's many farmers markets, Naschmarkt is *the* culinary medina. Wooden stalls crammed with food shops, snack, spice and vegetable stands and trendy restaurants all vie for attention as you make your way through the bustle. Come to stock up on picnic supplies or just chill with a bite at one of dining

spots – people-watching is part of the experience. See below for more on the Naschmarkt.

◉ THIRD MAN PRIVATE COLLECTION

☎ 586 48 72; 04, Pressgasse 25; adult/10-16yr €7.50/4; ⏱ 2-6pm Sat; ◉ U4 Kettenbrückengasse

Fans of the quintessential film set in post-WWII Vienna (voted best British film of the 20th century by the British Film Institute) will enjoy perusing the posters, *Third Man* paraphernalia and the rest of the 3000 or so objects on show here. Stills on the walls also illustrate the craftsmanship of Australian-born cameraman Robert Krasker, who received an Oscar for his work.

◉ WIEN MUSEUM

☎ 505 87 47-0; www.wienmuseum.at; 04, Karlsplatz 5; adult/under 19yr €6/free; ⏱ 10am-6pm Tue-Sun; ◉ U1, U2, U4 Karlsplatz ◉ D, 1, 2, 62 ◉ 4A

The Wien Museum provides an insightful snapshot of the development of Vienna from prehistory

---

NASCHMARKT ANTIQUES

In addition to the food and spice purveyors, the Naschmarkt hosts an antique *Flohmarkt* (flea market) from 6.30am to 6pm each Saturday. But before you decide to plonk down cash for that antique Biedermeier nightstand you simply *must* have for your bedroom, do some price comparisons and research. It may or may not be real and, if it is, it may well cost twice what it would at an antique shop in town. Nonetheless, browsing the stalls is a ball and the wares will surely stir your inner interior designer.

Antique hunters can scratch their itch at the *Flohmarkt* (flea market)

RICHARD NEBESKY

to the present day, putting the city and its personalities in a meaningful context. Highlights include a fascinating model of the city in its medieval heyday and a second model of the Innere Stadt showing the Ringstrasse developments.

🛍 SHOP

🛍 FAIR KLEIDUNG *Clothing*

☎ 599 35 27; 05, Kettenbrückengasse 3; 🕑 2-6pm Wed-Fri, 10am-4pm Sat; 🚌 59A

Handmade babies', children's and women's clothing in exquisite patterns dominate here – no two items are alike. All materials and workmanship is fair trade – most pieces are made by small, local designers.

🛍 FLO VINTAGE MODE *Fashion*

☎ 586 07 73; www.vintageflo.com; 04, Schleifmühlgasse 15a; 🕑 10am-6.30pm Mon-Fri, to 3.30pm Sat; 🚌 59A

In a city this enamoured with its glamorous past, it's no less than shocking that there are few true vintage clothing stores in town. The clothes here are fastidiously and beautifully displayed, from pearl-embroidered art nouveau masterpieces to 1950s and '60s New Look pieces and designer wear of the '70s and '80s (alphabetised Armani–Zegna). Prices (and quality) are high.

⌂ GABARAGE UPCYCLING DESIGN *Furniture, Accessories*

☎ 585 76 32 20; www.gabarage.at; 04, Schleifmühlgasse 6; ⏲ 10am-6pm Mon-Fri, to 3pm Sat; ⊟ 59A

Recycled design, ecology and social responsibility are the mottoes at gabarage upcycling design. Old sealing rings become earrings, former outdoor rubbish bins get a new life as tables and chairs, advertising tarpaulins morph into carry bags and fused ring binders reappear as recliners. Humans also receive a second shot at a new life: after completing substance abuse therapy, former addicts receive jobs plus one year's

Recycle, redesign, reuse – gabarage   KRZYSZTOF DYDYNSKI

training in various skills through gabarage's own occupational-therapy program.

⌂ GÖTTIN DES GLÜCKS
Clothing

☎ 358 74 15; www.goettindesgluecks.com; 04, Operngasse 32; ⏲ 12am-7pm Tue-Fri, 11am-6pm Sat; ⊟ 59A

Austria's first fair-fashion label conforms to the fair-trade model throughout the production process, through relationships with sustainable producers in India, Mauritius and beyond. This means supple, delicious cotton jerseys, skirts and shorts for men and women that manage the comfort of sleepwear in stylish, casual daywear. And yes, they also sell dreamy pyjamas (they'll make you want to indulge in a nap, pronto).

⌂ WIE WIEN *Accessories, Gifts*

☎ 0699-113 49 338; www.wiewien.at; 05, Kettenbrückengasse 5; ⏲ 2-7pm Mon-Fri, 11am-6pm Sat; ⊟ 59A

A Vienna concept store like no other – each piece in the shop represents the city in some way, from delicate ceramics with a Riesenrad (giant Ferris wheel) stencilled upon them, to colouring books filled with Vienna scenes, whimsical buttons and T-shirts depicting the Naschmarkt, the Stephansdom and other landmarks.

Karl Emilio-Pircher & Fidel Peugot
Designers, and founders of Walking-Chair Design Studio (☎ 713 24 84 10; www.walking-chair.com; Rasumofskygasse 10; ⊙ 9am-6pm Mon-Fri)

How did the name walking chair come about, and how does your work reflect Viennese design? Karl actually built a chair that walks! It's based on the idea that a chair – or any piece of furniture – has a soul and a personality. We are creators and inventors, furniture is functional but also a work of art. This is also the philosophy behind much of the design scene in Vienna. It fuses traditional details with modern, stylish elements. **What is inspiring about this city?** Vienna is a multicultural city and there isn't too much stress, which allows for a certain amount of mental freedom. This opens up multiple possibilities and options, which is crucial for creative design. And the design scene is slowly growing. **Where can visitors find some of your designs?** Right in front of Schloss Schönbrunn (p117). Our take on the classic public bench has recently been placed in front of the palace. The incongruent angles of each piece functions as a table, seat and counter. They're bright red and modern – you can't miss them. **Where do you recommend people go to get a feel for the design scene in the capital?** Definitely the Hofmobiliendepot (p58), one of the most extraordinary furniture collections in the world. **And to unwind in style?** The Loos American Bar (p52). It's simply magical. Most people think Loos covered it in mirrors to make it seem larger, but actually it's because he felt that people's thoughts should be free.

🍴 EAT

🍴 AROMAT *International* €€

☎ 913 24 53; 04, Margaretenstrasse 52; menu €7.90, mains €10-15; ⏲ 5-11pm Tue-Sun, closed mid-Jul–Aug; 🚌 59

The mainstay of this funky little eatery is fusion cooking with a strong emphasis on Upper Austrian and Vietnamese cuisine, but the menu changes daily. The charming decor features an open kitchen, simple formica tables, 1950s fixtures, a blackboard menu and a huge glass frontage. Personable staff help to create a convivial, barlike atmosphere.

🍴 BEOGRAD *Serbian* €€

☎ 587 74 44; 04, Schikanedergasse 7; mains €8.90-19.10; ⏲ 11.30am-2am Thu-Tue; 🚇 U4 Kettenbrückengasse 🚋 1, 62

Half of the pictures on the wall hang crooked, but that's the charm of Beograd's eccentric Balkan experience. There are roses on the tables, a piano, a violinist scratching away at his instrument and a wiry fellow gliding about squeezing out sounds from his harmonium. Servings are generous and the ingredients fresh and top quality. They do a good *ćevapčići* (Balkan grilled mince-meat dish).

🍴 DO-AN *Cafe* €

☎ 585 82 53; 06, Naschmarkt 412; breakfast €5-7, salads €4.80-6.60; ⏲ 7am-midnight Mon-Sat; 🚇 U4 Kettenbrückengasse; 🅥

Another rectangular aquarium with huge glass walls in the heart of Naschmarkt, Do-An does an eclectic mix of sandwiches, rice and noodle dishes, delicious salads and meats, as well as some Turkish staples, at affordable prices. Do-An enjoys a steadfast following that enjoys the relaxed vibe and sunny corners.

🍴 GERGELY'S *Steak* €€

☎ 544 07 67; 05, Schlossgasse 21; mains €15-30; ⏲ 6pm-1am Tue-Sat; 🚇 U4 Pilgramgasse

Set inside a 14th-century vaulted cellar, this local fave exclusively serves steaks made from quality beef sourced locally and internationally. There's a steak with a provenance and size for everyone, which you can enjoy with a strong selection of sauces and accompaniments. In summer, don't miss the garden, replete with a tractor, and lovely trees and seating.

🍴 NASCHMARKT DELI *American* €

☎ 585 08 23; 04, Naschmarkt 421; sandwiches €4-7, mains €6-12; ⏲ 7am-midnight Mon-Sat; 🚇 U4 Kettenbrückengasse

Among the many enticing stands in Naschmarkt, this deli has an edge on the others for its delicious sandwiches, falafel wraps, big baguettes, quick soups (lentil soup is a good bet) and heady array of breakfasts. On Saturday mornings this glass box overflows with punters waiting in anticipation for the Continental or English breakfast.

🍴 NENI *Middle Eastern, Israeli* €€
☎ 585 20 20; 06, Naschmarkt 510; breakfast €4-8.50, salads & snacks €4-11, mains €9-15; ☽ 8am-midnight Mon-Sat; ⓜ U4 Kettenbrückengasse 🚌 57A; Ⓥ
Some of Naschmarkt's 'stands' take on the proportions of Belvedere. Neni is no exception. Tasty delights range from caramelised aubergine with ginger and chilli (€9) served with expertly prepared lamb chops, or try the truffle-laced polenta (€14) or a pulse ragout with cranberries and rice (€9.50). Breakfast is served until 2pm; reserve ahead for dinner.

🍴 ON *Asian* €€
☎ 585 49 00; 05, Wehrgasse 8; lunch menu €7.50-8.50, mains €9-16.30; ☽ noon-midnight Mon-Sat, to 10.30pm Sun; 🚌 59A
ON is the best Austro-Asian fusion restaurant in this area of town. The ambience is relaxed and staff young and friendly. The menu spans *neo-Beisl* fare such as chicken liver with chilli, *gan-bien* (fried) beef strips or trout with ginger. The menu changes according to season and the whim of the

chef. The small, private garden is lovely in summer.

🍴 RESTAURANT COLLIO
Italian €€€
☎ 589 18 82; 04, Wiedener Hauptstrasse 12; 2-course lunch €15, 5-course €48.90, mains €11.90-24.90; ☽ noon-2.30pm & 6.30-10pm Mon-Fri, 6.30-10pm Sat; ⓜ U4 Kettenbrückengasse, Karlsplatz 🚋 1, 62; ✕ Ⓥ
This Sir Terence Conran–designed restaurant (inside Hotel Triest) is loungey, with mellow sounds trickling out of the speakers and parquet floor offset by the browns of padded benches. Collio changes its menu by season, and in a cold February you might find duck with fig mustard and fried polenta (€17.90) to warm the soul. Its focus is Venetian, but it wades across a broad culinary lagoon.

🍴 SILBERWIRT *Neo-Beisl* €€
☎ 544 4907; 05, Schlossgasse 21; mains €7.40-14.50; ☽ noon-midnight; ⓜ U4 Pilgramgasse; Ⓥ
This atmospheric *neo-Beisl* offers traditional Viennese cuisine using mostly organic and local produce. *Wiener Schnitzel* (€13.40), local trout with pumpkin-seed butter and fresh herbs (€12.80) and Styrian corn-fed chicken drumstick (€8.40) are complemented by some liver, vegetarian and Austrian noodle dishes. In summer, hit

the garden area – it's one of the best in Vienna.

🍴 TANCREDI *Neo-Beisl*   €€
☎ 941 00 48; 04, Grosse Neugasse 5; lunch menu €7.50-15, mains €7.80-19.80; 🕙 11.30am-2.30pm & 6pm-midnight Tue-Sat, 11.30am-2.30pm Mon; 🚃 62; Ⓥ

This former *Beisl* serves lovingly prepared regional and fish specialities, seasonal fare, organic dishes and an extensive range of Austrian wines. The harmonious surroundings are the icing on the cake: warm, pastel-yellow walls, stripped-back wooden floors, fittings from yesteryear and a tree-shaded garden that fills up quickly in summer.

🍴 UMAR *Fish*   €€
☎ 587 04 56; 04, Naschmarkt 76; midday menu €12-13, mains €13-30;

WORTH THE TRIP: TICHY ICE CREAM

It only takes one lick of **Tichy** (☎ 604 44 46; 10, Reumannplatz 13; 🕙 10am-11pm mid-Mar-Sep; Ⓜ U1 Reumannplatz) ice cream and you're hooked. In addition to the usual creamy suspects, this legendary *Eissalon* (ice-cream parlour) is known for pioneering *Eismarillenknödel* (ball of vanilla ice cream with apricot centre). It's a mere cone's throw away from the U-Bahn station – just look for Tichy's loyal patrons scattered around on park benches, grinning and enjoying their sweet treats. And be prepared to shove your way through crowds to reach the counter – it's all part of the fun.

© SUZANNE LONG / ALAMY

🕐 **11am-midnight Mon-Sat;** ⓜ **U1, U2, U4 Karlsplatz**

One of the best fish restaurants in Vienna, Umar serves seafood imported from Italy and Turkey at its large Naschmarkt stall. Choose between whole fish, mussels in white-wine sauce and giant shrimps fried in herb butter.

🍴 **URBANEK** *Austrian*   €

☎ 587 20 80; 04, Naschmarkt 46; ham with bread €3.60; 🕐 9am-6.30pm Mon-Thu, from 8am Fri, 7.30am-4pm Sat; ⓜ U1, U2, U4 Karlsplatz; ✕

Step inside Urbanek and enter a world of the finest cuts of (mainly organic) cured meats – smoked, salted, cooked or raw. There's scarcely enough room to swing a cat inside and the atmosphere is rarefied but relaxed as you ponder the exquisite cheeses and delicately cut slices of Mangalitza pig – a woolly variety prized for its delicious ham.

🍴 **ZUM ALTEN FASSL** *Beisl*   €€

☎ 544 42 98; 05, Ziegelofengasse 37; midday menu €5.70-6.80, mains €7.50-13.90; 🕐 11.30am-3pm & 5pm-1am Mon-Fri, 5pm-1am Sat, noon-3pm & 5pm-midnight Sun; 🚌 13A

With its private garden amid residential houses, and its polished wooden interior (typical of a well-kept *Beisl*), Zum Alten Fassl is worth the trip just for a drink. But

Viennese favourites and regional specialities, such as *Eierschwammerl* (chanterelle mushrooms) and *Blunzengröstl* (blood sausage with fried potato) are worth lingering for. And look for the Falco plaque – between 1974 and 1982 the singer lived upstairs.

🍸 DRINK

🍸 **CAFÉ RÜDIGERHOF**

Coffee House

☎ 586 31 38; 05, Hamburgerstrasse 20; 🕐 9am-2am; ⓜ U4 Kettenbrückengasse

Rüdigerhof's facade is a glorious example of *Jugendstil* (art nouveau) architecture, and the furniture and fittings inside could be straight out of an *I Love Lucy* set. The atmosphere is homely and familiar and the terrace huge and shaded. On Saturday mornings it fills up quickly with Naschmarkt shoppers.

🍸 **KUNSTHALLENCAFÉ** *Bar, Cafe*

☎ 587 00 73; 04, Treitlstrasse 2; 🕐 10am-2am; ⓜ U1, U2, U4 Karlsplatz 🚋 D, 1, 2 🚌 59A, 62

The Kunsthallencafé carries plenty of 'cool' clout and attracts a relaxed and arty crowd. The big sofas go quickly, but there are plenty of small tables that are perfect for an intimate evening. In summer the terrace (with more couches) is one enormous outdoor lounge.

▼ ORANGE ONE *Bar*

☎ 586 22 20; 04, Margaretenstrasse 26; ⏰ from 4pm; 🚌 59A

Orange One boasts a modern bar with a distinct retro feel and grown-up attitude. DJs play most nights and off-beat films are intermittently projected on the back wall. If smoke is a problem, it's best not to spend too much time here on winter nights.

▼ SCHIKANEDER *Bar*

☎ 585 58 88; 04, Margareten Strasse 22-24; ⏰ 6pm-4am; 🚌 59A

Most of the colour in Schikaneder comes from the regularly projected movies splayed across one of its white walls – the students and arty crowd who frequent this grungy bar dress predominantly in black. But that's not to detract from the bar's atmosphere, which exudes energy well into the wee small hours of the morning. Schikaneder (opposite) also hosts movies most nights.

▼ SEKT COMPTOIR *Wine Bar*

☎ 432 53 88; www.sektcomptoir.at; 04, Schleifmühlgasse 19; ⏰ 4-10pm Mon-Fri, 10am-5pm Sat; 🚌 59A

Szigeti vineyards (a leading producer of Austrian Sekt – sparkling wine – in Burgenland) serves its own brand only at this tiny, wood-panelled wine bar. Shoppers with bulging grocery bags from nearby Naschmarkt often spill onto the sidewalk, enjoying a tipple or four.

Sekt Comptoir: little elbow room, lots of elbow exercise

KRZYSZTOF DYDYNSKI

It rarely offers much elbow room, but the bubbly spirit of the place is so intoxicating most just chuckle and squish with a wide grin.

⭐ PLAY

⭐ GOODMANN *Club*
☎ 967 44 15; www.goodmann.at; 04, Rechte Wienzeile 23; 🕙 3am-10am Mon-Fri, to noon Sat & Sun; Ⓜ U4 Kettenbrückengasse 🚌 59A

A tiny place attracting clubbers who want to dance into the morning, Goodmann serves food upstairs (until 8am) and hides its night owls, who are an eclectic mix of old and young (but always in a merry state), downstairs.

⭐ RADIOKULTURHAUS
Concert Venue
☎ 501 70 377; www.radiokulturhaus.orf.at, in German; 04, Argentinierstrasse 30a; tickets €15-25; 🕙 box office 2pm until 30 min before performance Mon-Fri, to 1hr before performance Sat & Sun, cafe 9am-midnight Mon-Fri, performance times Sat & Sun; Ⓜ U1 Taubstummengasse 🚌 D

Expect anything from odes to Sinatra and REM to an evening dedicated to Beethoven and

Mozart at the Radiokulturhaus. This is one of Vienna's cultural hot spots and the venue also presents dance, lectures, literary readings, and low-key performances in its cafe.

⭐ ROXY *Club*
☎ 961 88 00; www.roxyclub.at; 04, Operngasse 24; 🕙 11pm-4am Thu-Sat; Ⓜ U1, U2, U4 Karlsplatz 🚌 59A

A seminal club for years, Roxy still manages to run with the clubbing pack, and sometimes leads the way. DJs from Vienna's electronica scene regularly guest on the turntables and most nights it's hard to find a space on the small dance floor. Expect a crowded, but very good, night out here.

⭐ SCHIKANEDER *Cinema*
☎ 585 28 67; www.schikaneder.at, in German; 04, Margaretenstrasse 24; 🚌 59A

Located next to the bar of the same name, Schikaneder is the darling of Vienna's alternative-cinema scene. The film subject range is quite broad but also highly selective, and art house through and through.

BELVEDERE TO THE CANAL

Designed by Johann Lukas von Hildebrandt, Belvedere Palace (Schloss Belvedere) is one of the world's finest baroque palaces. It was built for the brilliant military strategist Prince Eugene of Savoy, conqueror of the Turks in the Austro-Turkish War of 1716–18 and hero to a nation. The Unteres (Lower) Belvedere was built first (1714–16), with an orangery attached, and was the prince's summer residence. Connected to it by a long, land-scaped garden is the Oberes (Upper) Belvedere (1721–23), the venue for the prince's banquets and other big bashes.

Heading northeast of the Belvedere you hit the Danube Canal and the Hundertwasserhaus, Vienna's most famous residential building, designed by Austria's quirky Friedensreich Hundertwasser. Southeast of here brings several sights scattered far apart: the Gasometer, the quintessential mark of Viennese modern architecture; and three equally fascinating cemeteries. Two are famous for the composers, intellectuals and artists buried there; the other is full of unmarked graves, but is well remembered by fans of Richard Linklater's independent film *Before Sunrise*.

BELVEDERE TO THE CANAL

◉ SEE

◉ BELVEDERE PALACE: OBERES BELVEDERE

☎ 795 57-0; www.belvedere.at; 03, Prinz-Eugen-Strasse 27; adult/child under 19 €9.50/free; ⏱ 10am-6pm; 🚋 D

Oberes Belvedere is the pinnacle of Belvedere Palace (Schloss Belvedere). The museum's collection offers a deep insight into Austrian artists, and the baroque palace is a masterpiece whose interior allows you to drift with the ebb and flow of the ages, from the historic to the modern. Herculean figures supporting columns greet you in its lobby and the exploits of Alexander the Great flank its stairs. Highlights are Gustav Klimt's *The Kiss* (1908) and *Judith* (1901), and Biedermeier works by Ferdinand Georg Waldmüller (1793–1865) and modern artists of the calibre of Hans Makart (1840–84), Friedensreich Hundertwasser (1928–2000), Fritz Wotruba (1907–75) and many more. While visiting the Upper Belvedere, don't miss the elaborately stuccoed and frescoed **Marmorsaal** (Marble Hall), which offers superb views over the palace gardens and Vienna.

◉ BELVEDERE PALACE: PALACE GARDENS

03, Rennweg/Prinz-Eugen-Strasse; 🚋 D, 71

The long garden between the two Belvederes is laid out in classical

98

BELVEDERE COMBINED TICKETS

The Belvedere is home to the **Österreichische Galerie** (Austrian Gallery), split between the Unteres Belvedere and the Orangery, which combine to house special exhibitions, and the Oberes Belvedere. A **combined ticket** (adult/under 19yr €14/ free) allows entry to **Oberes Belvedere**, **Unteres Belvedere**, the **Orangery**, **Prunkstall**, **Augarten Contemporary** (p105) and the **Prunkräume**, and is valid for more than one day.

French style and has sphinxes and other mythical beasts along its borders. It's an excellent antidote to museum fatigue and is worth a visit on its own for its small **Alpine Garden** (adult/concession €3.20/2.50; ⏱ 10am-6pm Apr-Jul), which contains 3500 plant species and a bonsai section, and its much larger **Botanic Gardens** (admission free; ⏱ 9am-1hr before dusk). Opening times of the garden vary almost monthly. Core hours are from 6.30am to at least 8pm from March to mid-August, and to at least 6pm the rest of the year.

◉ BELVEDERE PALACE: UNTERES BELVEDERE

☎ 795 57-0; www.belvedere.at; 03, Rennweg 6; adult/under 19yr €9.50/free; ⏱ 10am-6pm Thu-Tue, to 9pm Wed; 🚋 71

Built between 1714 and 1716, the Lower Belvedere is a treat of ba-

A royal feast of art, gardens and architecture at Belvedere Palace

KRZYSZTOF DYDYNSKI

roque delights. Highlights include Prince Eugene's former residential apartment and ceremonial rooms, the **Groteskensaal** (Hall of the Grotesque, now the museum shop), a second **Marmorsaal** (Marble Hall), the **Marmorgalerie** (Marble Gallery) and the **Goldenes Zimmer** (Golden Room). Temporary exhibitions are held here and in the redesigned **Orangery**, which has a walkway with views over Prince Eugene's private garden and to Oberes Belvedere.

GASOMETER
www.wiener-gasometer.at; 10, Guglgasse 6-14; 🚇 **U3 Gasometer**
These four 75m-tall, round gas containers supplied gas to the city from 1899 to 1969. But in the 1990s they were redeveloped by several architectural groups into 615 apartments, a students' hostel, and a leisure and shopping complex. Today they represent one of the best examples of Viennese modern architecture.

HUNDERTWASSER HAUS
03, Löwengasse/Kegelgasse; 🚋 **1, 0**
This Hundertwasser-designed residential block of flats is one of Vienna's most fantastical landmarks. It's not possible to see inside the colourful facade and gold onion domes, but you can visit the shopping and dining complex, **Kalke Village** (www.kalke-village.at;

Dr Agnes Husslein-Arco
Director of Belvedere Museum, in the Oberes Belvedere (p98)

What is your primary role at the Belvedere? I'm like a conductor, making sure the collection comes together in a gorgeous symphony of art.
What's the most inspiring element of the Belvedere? The palace itself is captivating – it's no surprise it's considered one of Europe's finest baroque structures. **If you only have one afternoon, what's on your 'don't miss' list?** The Oberes Belvedere. It gives you a straight overview of the icons in our Austria Collection – this includes several signature pieces by Gustav Klimt. **And after seeing the country's great artists, what's next on your favourite palace itinerary?** In winter, stop off for a coffee at the **Belvedere Cafe** (☎ 798 88 88; Oberes Belvedere; ⏱ 10am-6pm). Try the traditional *Wiener Melange* (Viennese speciality coffee) or the Klimt, which is served with amaretto and cream. On a warm day, a walk across the palace gardens from the Oberes Belvedere to the Unteres Belvedere is delightful, and takes you right into Schwarzenbergplatz and the centre of the city.

STOLEN TREASURES

In 1938 many Jewish families were forced to flee Austria, and the Nazis seized their property. The Bloch-Bauers were one such family, and among their substantial fortune were five Klimt originals, including the *Portrait of Adele Bloch-Bauer I* (1907).

The paintings hung in the Oberes Belvedere until early 2006 when a US Supreme Court ruled the Austrian government must return the paintings to their rightful owner, Adele Bloch's niece and heir, Maria Altmann. Austria believed it was entitled to the paintings because Adele Bloch, who died in 1925, had specified that they be donated to the national gallery. However, her husband, who died in exile in 1945, wanted them returned to his family.

The paintings arrived in the US to much joy, while Austria mourned the loss of part of its cultural heritage. The government was offered the chance to buy the paintings, but the US$100 million price tag was regarded as too steep. It later proved to have been a bargain asking price – the *Portrait of Adele Bloch-Bauer I*, alone, fetched US$135 million at auction, at the time the highest price paid for a painting. It now hangs in the New York Neue Galerie, a museum devoted to German and Austrian art.

☼ 9am-7pm), across the street – it's also the handiwork of the radical architect, and features colourful ceramics and a distinct absence of straight lines.

◉ KUNSTHAUSWIEN
☎ 712 04 95; www.kunsthauswien. com; 03, Untere Weissgerberstrasse 13; adult/11-18yr €9/4.50; ☼ 10am-7pm; 🚋 1, 0

This art house, with its bulging ceramics, lack of straight lines and colourful tilework, is another of Hundertwasser's inventive creations. It is something of a paean to Hundertwasser, illustrating his paintings, graphics, tapestry, philosophy, ecology and architecture. Be sure to wander to the rooftop where you'll find a shady patch of grass under the grove of trees.

◉ NAMENLOSEN FRIEDHOF
☎ 0664-623 56 64; 11, Alberner Hafen; 🚌 76A

The Cemetery of the Nameless was established in 1900 to bury the grey, unknown dead (often suicides or accident victims) who washed up on the shores of the Danube. But it's most well known as one of the places where the two protagonists, Céline and Jesse (played by Julie Delpy and Ethan Hawke), spend time in the film *Before Sunrise*.

◉ ST MARXER FRIEDHOF
03, Leberstrasse 6-8; ☼ 7am-7pm Jun-Aug, to 6pm May & Sep, to 5pm Apr & Oct, to dusk Nov-Mar; 🚋 71 🚌 74A

The Cemetery of St Marx is a pilgrimage site for Mozart aficionados – the composer was buried here in an unmarked grave. Over time the site was forgotten and his wife's search for the exact location was in vain. But a poignant memorial (Mozartgrab) made from a broken pillar and a discarded stone angel was erected in the area where he was most likely laid to rest.

⊙ ZENTRALFRIEDHOF

☎ 760 41-0; 11, Simmeringer Hauptstrasse 232-244; admission free; ☒ info office 8am-3pm Mon-Sat, cemetery 7am-8pm May-Aug, to 7pm Apr & Sep, to 6pm Mar & Oct, 8am-5pm Nov-Feb; ☒ 6, 71 Opened in 1874, the Central Cemetery has grown to include 2.5 million graves, far exceeding Vienna's current population. It contains tombs to Vienna's greats, including composers Beethoven, Schubert, Brahms, Schönberg and the whole Strauss clan, architects Theophil von Hansen and Adolf Loos, and *the* man of Austrian pop, Falco (Hans Hölzel). The information office is at gate 2.

🍴 EAT

🍴 GASTHAUS WILD *Neo-Beisl* €€

☎ 920 94 77; 03, Radetzkyplatz 1; midday menu €7.50, mains €8.80-17.50; ☒ 9am-1am; ☒ 1, 0; Ⓥ
Gasthaus Wild, formerly a dive of a *Beisl* (small tavern), has in recent years morphed into a great *neo-Beisl*. Its dark, wood-panelled inte-

rior retains a traditional look, and the menu includes favourites such as *Gulasch* (goulash) and *Schnitzel mit Erdäpfelsalat* (schnitzel with potato salad), but also veal filet with dumplings spiced with blood sausage. The menu changes regularly, the ambience is relaxed, the staff welcoming and the wine selection good.

🍴 KIANG *Asian* €€

☎ 715 34 70; 03, Landstrasse Hauptstrasse 50; mains €11.20-17.80, sushi & sashimi €11.80-19.50, light mains €5.40-7.80; ☒ 11.30am-3pm & 6.30-11.30pm; ☻ U3 Rochusgasse; Ⓥ
This ultramodern pan-Asian restaurant near Rochusplatz is a relaxed and spacious experience where you can enjoy excellent sushi and sashimi. *Sha cha* noodle soup with beef costs €10.80, and in summer there's outdoor seating. A Mongolian lamb dish (served with pitta bread), Chinese, Thai and Japanese dishes also figure on the menu.

🍴 RESTAURANT INDUS

Indian, Pakistani €€
☎ 713 43 44; 03, Radetzkystrasse 20; mains €11.50-15; ☒ 11.30am-2.30pm & 6-11pm Mon-Fri & Sun, 6-11pm Sat; ☒ 1, 0; Ⓥ
Indus' Martin Hess–designed interior is as pleasing as its exceptional food and atmosphere.

A *saag gosht* (lamb and spinach curry) costs €11.90, and can be enjoyed in the garden out the back if the sloped, jagged ceiling and light interior doesn't keep you inside.

TRZESNIEWSKI *Sandwiches* €
☎ 715 28 19; 03, Rochusmarkt 8-9; bread with spread per 100g from €2.80; ⏲ 8.30am-7pm Mon-Fri, to 5pm Sat; Ⓜ U3 Rochusgasse; Ⓥ
Possibly the finest sandwich shop in Austria, Trzesniewski has been serving spreads and breads to the entire spectrum of munchers (Kafka was a regular here) for more than 100 years. Choose from 21 delectably thick spreads – paprika, tuna with egg, salmon and Swedish herring are but a few examples – for your choice of bread, or simply pick a selection from those waiting ready made.

DRINK

SALM BRÄU *Microbrewery*
☎ 799 59 92; www.salmbraeu.com; 03, Rennweg 8; ⏲ 11am-midnight; 🚋 71
Right next to Belvedere Palace, this convivial beer hall brews its own *Helles*, *Pils*, *Märzen*, *G'mischt* and *Weizen*. Happy hour is from 3pm to 5pm Monday to Friday and noon to 4pm Saturday.

Good times are brewing at Salm Bräu ᴷᴿᶻᵞˢᶻᵀᴼᶠ ᴰᵞᴰᵞᴺˢᴷᴵ

PLAY
KONZERTHAUS *Concert Venue*
☎ 242 002; www.konzerthaus.at; 03, Lothringerstrasse 20; tickets €12-120; ⏲ box office 9am-7.45pm Mon-Fri, to 1pm Sat; Ⓜ U4 Stadtpark 🚋 4A
The Konzerthaus is a major venue in classical music circles, but during the year ethnic music, rock, pop or jazz can be heard in its hallowed halls. Up to three simultaneous performances – in the Grosser Saal, the Mozart Saal and the Schubert Saal – can be staged; this massive complex also features another four concert halls.

LEOPOLDSTADT TO DONAUPARK

The western edge of Leopoldstadt (district 2) hugs the Innere Stadt, but while separated only by the slim Danube Canal, they feel worlds apart.

The definition of quiet gentrification, Leopoldstadt is seeing an eruption of bohemian and trendy nightlife and restaurants, including around the multiethnic Karmelitermarkt, where Muslims and Jews set up shop side by side. But it's also Vienna's favourite area for getting outdoors for some old-fashioned, fresh-air fun. The Augarten parkland carves its way into the area's northern edge, while to the southeast lies the Prater's 60 sq km of woodland park. Viennese flock to the Prater to stroll or cycle tree-shaded alleys, or simply soak up the sun in the park's open fields.

The Prater is also home to the Würstelprater, an amusement park with rides that could easily date from the early 20th century, which is dominated by the red cabins of the Riesenrad, one of the world's most famous Ferris wheels.

Northeast of the Prater sits Donauinsel (Danube Island), a skinny strip of land dividing the Danube River from the Neue Donau (New Danube). East of

LEOPOLDSTADT TO DONAUPARK

Please see over for map

Donauinsel lies Donaustadt and Donaupark. This ear-shaped swath of land is surrounded by a crescent of water, the Alte Donau (Old Danube) – an arm long cut off from the main river. It's dotted with river beaches – boasting water sports galore – and kilometres of walking, cycling, and in-line-skating tracks. Donaustadt is home to the UN in Vienna and Donaupark, which sprouts both trees and Vienna's tallest structure, the Donauturm.

◉ SEE

◉ AUGARTEN

www.kultur.park.augarten.org, in German; 03, Obere Augartenstrasse; 🕐 6am-dusk Apr-Oct, from 6.30am Nov-Mar; 🚇 31 🚊 5A

This meadow-dotted park, criss-crossed by tree-lined paths, is Leopoldstadt's most vibrant green space. While it serves as a home for the porcelain factory (p110), art exhibitions (below) and summer fave Kino Unter Sternen (p113), it's most captivating features are the austere **Flaktürme** (flak towers). Built from 1943 to 1944 as a defence against air attacks and to house troops, a hospital and a munitions factory, these bare monolithic blocks stand like sleeping giants among the residential districts of Vienna.

◉ AUGARTEN CONTEMPORARY/GUSTINUS AMBROSI-MUSEUM

☎ 216 86 16 21; www.belvedere.at; 02, Scherzergasse 1a; adult €5/3.50; 🕐 11am-7pm Thu-Sun; 🚊 2, 5

Sculptures by Austrian-born Gustinus Ambrosi (1893–1975) are the highlight of the works displayed inside the Atelier section of this museum. Alongside his works are sculptures by other European artists from the 20th and 21st centuries. The Augarten Contemporary, part of the same museum, features temporary exhibits from international artists – check the program on the website. Entry to the Atelier is included in the Belvedere Palace ticket (see the boxed text, p98).

◉ DONAUTURM

☎ 263 35 72; www.donauturm.at; 22, Donauturmstrasse 4; adult/under 14yr €5.90/4.30; 🕐 10am-10pm; 🚇 U1 Kaisermühlen Vienna International Centre 🚌 20B

At 252m, the Donauturm (Danube Tower) in Donaupark is Vienna's tallest structure. Its revolving

---

RIESENRAD COMBINED TICKETS

Various combination tickets for the giant Ferris wheel exist, but the best value are Riesenrad plus Tiergarten Schönbrunn (adult/child €16.50/7) and Riesenrad plus Donauturm (€11/6.10).

restaurant at 170m allows fantastic panoramic views of the whole city and beyond. The food tends to be tried and trusted Viennese favourites, and your view might even reveal a human figure swiftly plunging downward – adventurous types can bungee jump off the side of the tower (see the website for details).

JOHANN STRAUSS RESIDENCE

☎ 214 01 21; www.wienmuseum.at; 02, Praterstrasse 54; adult/under 19yr/concession €2/free/1; ☼ 10am-1pm & 2-6pm Tue-Sun; ◉ U1 Nestroyplatz ◼ 5A

Strauss the Younger called Praterstrasse 54 home from 1863 to 1878 and composed *the* waltz, 'The Blue Danube', under its high ceilings. Inside you'll find an above-average collection of Strauss and ballroom memorabilia, including an Amati violin said to have belonged to him and oil paintings from his last apartment, which was destroyed during WWII. The rooms are bedecked in period furniture from Strauss' era.

RIESENRAD

☎ 729 54 30; www.wienerriesenrad.com; 02, Prater 90; adult/3-14yr €8.50/3.50; ☼ 9am-11.45pm May-Sep, 10am-9.45pm Mar, Apr & Oct, 10am-7.45pm Nov-Feb; ◉ U1 Praterstern ◼ 0, 5, 21

Shoot your own scene on the Riesenrad

KRZYSZTOF DYDYNSKI

LEOPOLDSTADT'S JEWISH HERITAGE

Leopoldstadt started life as a walled Jewish ghetto in 1624 under the watchful eye of Ferdinand II, but the district gained its name from Leopold I. This notoriously anti-Semitic Habsburg expelled Jews from the area in 1670, destroyed their synagogue and replaced it with a church (Leopoldkirche). But by the 18th and 19th centuries, the city was once again experiencing an influx of immigrant Jews, particularly from Eastern Europe. The area saw overcrowding and some of the worst conditions in the city. During WWII, the Nazis expelled all Jews, and left behind a desolate district. The beginning of the 21st century has seen another new influx, and Jews now share Leopoldstadt with immigrants from Turkey and the Balkans. **Karmelitermarkt** (02, Im Werd; 6am-6.30pm Mon-Fri, to 2pm Sat; U2 Taborstrasse 2 5A), the district's busy and vibrant food market, is chock-full of kosher and halal food and is well worth a visit to glimpse the neighbourhood's ethnic diversity. Saturday includes an organic farmers market.

The Riesenrad (Ferris wheel) is a towering, modern symbol of Vienna. Built in 1897 by Englishman Walter B Basset, the wheel rises to 65m and takes about 20 minutes to rotate its 430-tonne weight one complete circle. This gives you ample time to snap some fantastic shots of the city and savour the ride. It survived bombing in 1945 (returning in good form, albeit with only half the cabins it held prewar) and achieved celluloid fame in *The Third Man* (in the scene where Holly Martins finally confronts Harry Lime), the James Bond flick *The Living Daylights* and director Richard Linklater's cult hit *Before Sunrise*. A ride on the Riesenrad includes entry into the **Panorama**, a collection of disused wheel-cabins filled with models depicting scenes from the city's history, including Roman Vienna and the Turkish invasions.

UNO-CITY

260 60 3328; www.unvienna.org; 22, Wagramer Strasse 5; adult/child/concession €6/2/4; tours 11am & 2pm Mon-Fri; U1 Kaisermühlen Vienna International Centre

Though home to a variety of international organisations, UNO-City (also known as Vienna International Centre) is dominated by the UN's third-largest office in the world. Tours take you through conference rooms and exhibitions on UN activities and add insight into what goes on behind doors that are usually closed. It may appear dated today, but the complex was the picture of modernism when it was built in 1979. It still holds a rather glamorous extraterritorial status – so bring your passport.

⊙ WIENER PORZELLANMANUFAKTUR AUGARTEN

☎ 211 24 200; www.augarten.at; 02, Obere Augartenstrasse 1, Schloss Augarten; tours adult/under 10yr/concession €12/3/6; ⏲ 9.30am-5pm Mon-Fri, tours 10am Mon-Fri; 🚋 31 🚌 5A

Vienna's Porcelain Factory, the second-oldest porcelain manufacturer in Europe, produces exquisite pieces featuring plenty of fanciful flourishes. One-hour tours of the premises explain the process of turning white kaolin, feldspar and quartz into delicate creations through the process of moulding, casting, luting, glazing and painting.

⊙ WÜRSTELPRATER AMUSEMENT PARK

☎ 728 05 16; www.prater.at; 02, Prater 90; rides €1-10; ⊖ U1 Praterstern 🚌 0, 5, 21

The world's oldest amusement park may be overshadowed by the Riesenrad, but beyond the famous wheel lie more than 200 fun-fair rides, from roller coasters to modern big dippers, merry-go-rounds and bumper cars, plus a haunted house, go karts, games rooms, and fast food and cotton-candy stands – all loudly beckon-

ing you to be a kid again. The park is open to walk through year-round, all rides are open from May to October, and selected rides are open throughout the year.

🛍 SHOP
🏠 GUTER STOFF

Accessories, Fashion

☎ 338 43 57; http://guterstoff.com, in German; 02, Glockengasse 8a; ⏲ 11am-1pm & 2-6pm Tue-Fri, 11am-1pm Sat; ⊖ U2 Taborstrasse

The name means Good Stuff, which it is: fair-trade clothing from a handful of labels, including Move At (leather wallets and bags handmade in Vienna), Earth Positive and Continental Clothing (both casual street garb). Or give your favourite T-with-a-tear a rebirth: they sell their own 'hole pimps' (patches) in a variety of styles, colours and shapes.

🏠 NAGY STRICKDESIGN

Fashion

☎ 925 13 74; 02, Krummbaumgasse 2-4; ⏲ 2-7pm Tue, Wed & Fri, to 8pm Thu & Sat; 🚌 5A

The stripy cotton and viscose knitwear here is both classic and up-to-the-minute, with flattering shapes, vivid colours and designs for hot and cold weather. There are also linen pants and skirts in a range of bright colours and casual styles.

🍴 EAT

🍴 RESTAURANT VINCENT

International   €€€

☎ 214 15 16; 02, Grosse Pfarrgasse 7; mains €20-30, 10-course menu €98; 🕙 6pm-midnight Mon-Sat; Ⓓ U2 Taborstrasse 🚋 2 🚌 5A; 🍴

This Michelin-star stalwart serves an exceptional range of dishes based on seasonal produce. It focuses on classics, such as expertly prepared lamb, beef or poultry and pheasant, with occasional diversions, such as locally produced snails. Vincent's ambience is historic and traditional (but avoid the bland back room).

🍴 SCHÖNE PERLE

Neo-Beisl   €

☎ 243 35 93; 02, Grosse Pfarrgasse 2; midday menu €7, mains €4-16; 🕙 noon-11pm Mon-Fri, 10am-11pm Sat & Sun; Ⓓ U2 Taborstrasse, 🚋 2, 🚌 5A; Ⓥ

Schöne Perle (beautiful pearl) has a simple look and serves everything from lentil soups to *Tafelspitz* (prime boiled beef) and vegetarian and fish mains – and all are created with organic produce. Wines are from Austria, as are the large array of juices.

🍴 SPEZEREI

Tapas, Mediterranean   €€

☎ 218 47 18; Karmeliterplatz 2; tapas €6.90-10.90; 🕙 11.30am-11pm Mon-Sat; Ⓓ U2 Taborstrasse 🚋 2 🚌 5A; Ⓥ

This small *Vinothek* (wine bar) and Mediterranean tapas place specialises in Spanish fish tapas, focaccia and panini, with quality wines (mostly from Austria) to wash them down. About a dozen wines can be drunk by the glass, and several hundred by the bottle, including four house varieties. In summer, the neighbourhood's bohemian types flock to its outdoor tables.

KRZYSZTOF DYDYNSKI
Spezerei, a taste of the Viennaterranean

CLASSIC VIENNESE FARE IN LEOPOLDSTADT

While the food scene is on the move east of the canal, classic fare for hearty appetites at midrange prices is not to be forgotten. Two of the best choices here are **Karl Kolarik's Schweizer Haus** (☎ 728 01 52; 02, Prater 116; mains €6.40-15.80; 11am-11pm; U1, U2 Praterstern/Wien Nord 5, 0), Vienna's premier address for pork hocks; and the **Lusthaus** (☎ 728 95 65; 02, Freudenau 254; mains €9-16; noon-11pm Mon, Tue, Thu & Fri, to 6pm Sat & Sun May-Sep, to 6pm Thu-Tue Oct-Apr; 77A;), a former Habsburg hunting lodge from which you can take a walk in the Prater for an evening of elegant ambience.

DRINK

BRICKS LAZY DANCEBAR
Bar, Club

☎ 216 37 01; www.bricks.co.at, in German; 02, Taborstrasse 38; 8pm-4am; U2 Taborstrasse 2

A cross between a bar and a dance spot, this retro, red-vinyl space attracts a mainly 20-something set. The dance floor is tiny but cosy, with DJs spinning anything from timeless dance classics from the last four decades to electric, indie and alternative beats. All cocktails are half price before 10pm daily and all night on Mondays.

TACHLES *Bar, Cafe Venue*

☎ 212 03 58; 02, Karmeliterplatz 1; 5pm-2am; U2 Taborstrasse 2;

Smack on the main square in up-and-coming Leopoldstadt, this bohemian cafe-bar attracts an intellectual and laid-back crowd of locals in a relaxed, wood-panelled setting. Small bites with a Slavic slant are on offer (*pierogi*, borscht) and it hosts occasional live music and readings – the last Thursday of each month features young musicians in their vast cellar space.

PLAY

ALTE DONAU *Riverside Activities*
22, Untere Alte Donau; U1 Alte Donau, U6 Untere Alte Donau

Separated from the Neue Donau by Donaustadt, the Alte Donau is the landlocked arm of the Danube. It carried the main flow of the river until 1875, when artificial flood precautions created the linear course of today's Danube. A favourite of Viennese sailors, boaters and swimmers, Alte Donau is best appreciated by hopping in or on the water – alongside the free access points are nearly a dozen bathing complexes and boat hire outfits, open from May to September.

⭐ DONAUINSEL *Riverside Activities*
22; Ⓤ U1 Donauinsel
Vienna's prime aquatic play-ground (swimming, boating, you name it), the svelte Donauinsel (Danube Island) stretches 21.5km from north to south and divides the Danube in two, creating the **Neue Donau** (New Danube), a sepa-rate arm from the main river. With concrete paths running the entire length, it's best explored by bike. In summer, a cluster of bars – collectively called Sunken City and Copa Cagrana near Reichs-brücke – buzz throughout the day and evening. In June, don't miss the **Donauinselfest** (Danube Island Festival; p23).

⭐ FLUC *Bar, Live Music Venue*
www.fluc.at, in German; 02, Praterstern 5; ⏱ 6pm-4am; Ⓤ U1, U2 Praterstern ⓡ 0, 5
Looking for all the world like a pre-fab schoolroom, Fluc is the closest Vienna's nightlife scene comes to anarchy – without the fear of physical violence. Black-clad students, smashed alcoholics, 30-something freelancers and the occasional TV celebrity all share the stripped-back venue without any hassle, and DJs or live acts play

MOVIES ALFRESCO
Each summer from mid-July to mid-August, the **Augarten** (p105) hosts **Kino Unter Sternen** (Cinema Under the Stars; ☎ 0800-664 040; www.kinountersternen.at, in German; 02, Augarten; ⓡ 2 🚌 5A), the highly popular outdoor cinema, in the shadow of one of Augarten's Flaktürme. Films are an eclectic mix of classics and many are screened in their original language with German subtitles.

every night (electronica features heavily).

⭐ PRATERSAUNA *Club*
☎ 729 19 27; www.pratersauna.tv; 02, Waldsteingartenstrasse 135; ⏱ 10pm-6am Fri & Sat Jan-Apr, 9pm-6am Wed-Sun May-Sep; Ⓤ U1, U2 Praterstern
Pool, cafe, bistro and club con-verge in a former sauna – these days, you'll sweat it up on the dance floor. Any given night hosts light installations and perform-ance art to check out before or after you groove to electronica spun by international DJs. On warm nights it all spills out into the terrace, gardens and pool – if you need to cool down, nobody bats an eye if you take a quick dip.

SCHLOSS SCHÖNBRUNN & AROUND

In terms of displays of imperial wealth, Schloss Schönbrunn and its adjoining garden are second only to Versailles. Commissioned by Leopold I and designed by Johann Bernhard Fischer von Erlach, the original plans were hugely ambitious and aimed to dwarf the scale and opulence of Versailles. The imperial purse winced, however, and a 'less elaborate' building was finished in 1700, and named after the Schöner Brunnen (beautiful fountain) in its grounds.

At first glance, visitors could be forgiven for thinking the palace is all that's worth seeing, but beyond the grand walls lie equally impressive grounds. Besides the fountain, you'll find a maze, cemetery and palm house in a leisurely stroll around the exquisitely manicured gardens, which extend 1.2km east to west and 1km north to south.

To the west of the palace and gardens lies Hietzing, the posh residential neighbourhood that is home to upper class Viennese, a suitably lavish beer garden and a coffee house where the young Herr Strauss once performed. From here, a short hop on a tram whisks you southwest to the nearby winegrowing suburb of Mauer and its cluster of convivial *Heurigen* (wine taverns).

SCHLOSS SCHÖNBRUNN & AROUND

◉ SEE
Hietzinger Friedhof 1 A4
Kindermuseum 2 C2
Palmenhaus 3 A2
Schloss Schönbrunn 4 C2
Schloss Schönbrunn
    Gardens 5 C1
Tiergarten 6 B2
Wagenburg 7 C1
Wüstenhaus 8 A2

🍴 EAT
Brandauer's
    Schlossbräu 9 A2
Quell 10 F1

🍸 DRINK
Café Domayer 11 A1
Café Gloriette 12 C4

★ PLAY
Breitenseer
    Lichtspiele 13 B1
Marionettentheater 14 C1
Orangery 15 D2
Reigen 16 B1
U4 ....17 F2

NEIGHBOURHOODS

SCHLOSS SCHÖNBRUNN & AROUND

SEE

HIETZINGER FRIEDHOF

☎ 877 31 07; 13, Maxingstrasse 15; admission free; ⏰ 7am-8pm May-Aug, 7am-7pm Apr & Sep, 7am-6pm Mar & Oct, 8am-5pm Nov-Feb; 🚇 10, 60 🚌 56B, 58B, 156B

Aficionados of Vienna's Secessionist movement will want to make the pilgrimage to the Hietzinger cemetery to pay homage to some of its greatest members. Klimt, Moser and Wagner are all buried here. Others buried in the cemetery include Engelbert Dollfuss, leader of the Austro-Fascists, who was assassinated in 1934, and composer Alban Berg.

KINDERMUSEUM

☎ 811 13 239; www.schoenbrunn. at/kinder, in German; 13, Schloss Schönbrunn; admission adult/under 19yr €6.50/4.90, tours €6.50/4.90; ⏰ 10am-5pm Sat & Sun, tours in German 10.30am, 1.30pm & 3pm; 🚇 U4 Schönbrunn, U4 Hietzing 🚇 10, 58 🚌 10A

Schönbrunn's Children's Museum gives kids a taste of imperialism. Activities and displays help them discover the day-to-day life of the Habsburg court, and once they've got the idea, they can don princely outfits and start ordering the serfs (parents) around. Other rooms are devoted to toys, natural science and archaeology. Tours are also available in English, by appointment.

PALMENHAUS

☎ 877 50 874 06; 13, Maxingstrasse 13b; adult/under 18yr €4/3; ⏰ 9.30am-6pm May-Sep, to 5pm Oct-Apr; 🚇 U4 Hietzing 🚇 10, 58, 60

Travellers from London may think they're experiencing déjà vu on seeing the Palmenhaus (Palm House). It was built in 1882 by Franz Segenschmid as a replica of the one at Kew Gardens. Inside

---

TICKETS FOR SCHLOSS SCHÖNBRUNN

If you plan to see several sights at Schönbrunn, it's worth purchasing one of its combined tickets in advance at www.schoenbrunn.at. Prices vary according to whether it's summer season (April to October) or winter. The summer-season **Classic Pass** (adult/under 19yr €17.90/10.90) is valid for a grand tour of Schloss Schönbrunn. It's also valid for visits to the Kronprinzengarten (Crown Prince Garden); Irrgarten and Labyrinth (Maze and Labyrinth); Gloriette with its viewing terrace; and Hofbackstube Schönbrunn (Court Bakery Schönbrunn), where there's a chance to watch apple strudel being made before enjoying the result with a cup of coffee. The **Gold Pass** (€36/18) adds the Tiergarten, Palmenhaus, Wüstenhaus and Wagenburg. The **Winter Pass** (€25/12) includes the Grand Tour, Tiergarten, Palmenhaus, Wüstenhaus, Wagenburg, Gloriette, and Maze and Labyrinth.

is a veritable jungle of tropical plants from around the world. A combined ticket for the Palmenhaus and Wüstenhaus (p120) costs €6 per person.

SCHLOSS SCHÖNBRUNN

☎ 811 13-0; www.schoenbrunn.at; 13, Schloss Schönbrunn; Imperial Tour (26 rooms) with audio adult/under 19yr €9.50/6.50, Grand Tour (40 rooms) with audio €12.90/8.90; Grand Tour with guide €14.40/9.90; ⏰ 8.30am-6pm Jul-Aug, to 5pm Apr-Jun & Sep-Oct, to 4.30pm Nov-Mar; ◉ U4 Schönbrunn, U4 Hietzing ☒ 10, 58 ☒ 10A

If you only have time to explore one palace during your visit, taking a peek into the quirks and habits of Austria's most illustrious family, the Habsburgs, is a must. Though a mere 40 of the 1441 grand rooms are open to the public, the tours provide an insight into the personalities and the opulence of the baroque age. One of our favourite rooms is the fantastical *Spiegelsalon* (Hall of Mirrors), where a six-year-old Mozart played his first royal concert for Maria Theresia in 1762, and afterwards leapt into her lap and kissed her. Unfortunately, the lavish *Grosse Galerie* (Great Gallery) is being restored until late 2012. Tickets are time-stamped; if there's

Schloss Schönbrunn, a gilt-edged peek into Habsburg privilege   HANNAH LEVY

117

SCHÖNBRUNN GARDEN STROLL

Schloss Schönbrunn's gardens – created by Frenchman Jean Trehet and given their baroque form by later masters – are as vast and spectacular as the palace itself.

Begin your walk at the **Crown Prince Garden (1)**, a whimsical kaleidoscope of magenta, yellow and green abutting Schönbrunn's west wing. Weave your way along the path leading towards the looming hill and the well house, anchored by the figure of Egeria at the **Schöner Brunnen** (Beautiful Fountain; **2**). The adjacent fake-but-fabulous **Roman ruins (3)** are most notable for the pool framed by a faux semi-circular arch of crumbling walls. Looking downhill from the ruins, turn left to see Neptune, accompanied by a cast of sea nymphs, sea horses and other mythological elements, at **Neptunbrunnen** (Neptune Fountain; **4**). This is the lower gardens' centrepiece. With the fountain behind you, turn left and then right, which will bring you to the maze. A nightmare for the navigationally challenged, this 630m-long **Maze** (adult/child €2.90/1.70; ☽ 9am-7pm Jul & Aug, to 6pm Apr-Jun & Sep, to 5pm Oct; **5**) is a classic design based on the original 1892 maze. Adjoining the maze is the **Labyrinth (6)**, a playground with a giant mirror kaleidoscope. Exit and turn right, meander along any path uphill to the majestic, hilltop **Gloriette (7)**. Here, from the rooftop terrace, look back towards the palace and you will see Vienna shimmering in the distance.

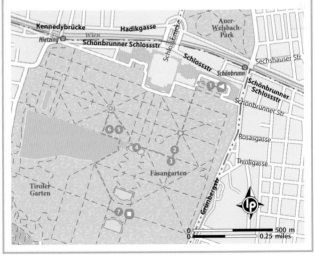

a lag before you can start, use the time to explore the gardens. See p10 for more on the palace.

◉ SCHLOSS SCHÖNBRUNN GARDENS

13, Schloss Schönbrunn; admission free; ☽ 6am-dusk Apr-Oct, from 6.30am Nov-Mar; ◉ U4 Schönbrunn, U4 Hietzing ▯ 10, 58 ▯ 10A

The beautifully tended formal gardens of the palace are a symphony of colour in the summer and a gentle combination of greys and browns in winter. The grounds were opened to the public by Joseph II in 1779 and are arranged according to a grid and star-shaped system. They hide numerous attractions,

including the riotous **Neptunbrunnen** (Neptune Fountain) and the **Schöner Brunnen** (Beautiful Fountain), from which the palace gained its name. Take a stroll around the gardens with our walking tour – see the boxed text, left.

◉ TIERGARTEN

☎ 877 92 94; www.zoovienna.at; 13, Maxingstrasse 13b; adult/child €14/6; ☽ 9am-6.30pm Apr-Sep, to 5.30pm Mar & Oct, to 5pm Feb, to 4.30pm Nov-Jan; ◉ U4 Hietzing ▯ 10, 58, 60

The oldest zoo in the world, Tiergarten Schönbrunn was founded by Franz Stephan in 1752 as a menagerie. It houses some 750 animals of all shapes and sizes,

---

EXPLORING THE LAINZER TIERGARTEN

At 25 sq km, the **Lainzer Zoo** (13, Hermesstrasse; admission free; ☽ 8am-dusk; ▯ 60B ▯ 60) is the largest and wildest of Vienna's city parks. While there's no traditional zoo in the park, you will encounter abundant wildlife, such as wild boar, deer, woodpeckers and squirrels. They freely inhabit the park, and the famous Lipizzaner horses spend their summers here. But the biggest draws are the extensive walking trails weaving their way through the lush woodland, and two key attractions: the **Hubertus-Warte** (508m), a viewing platform on top of Kaltbründlberg with sweeping views of Vienna, and the **Hermesvilla** (☎ 804 13 24; 13, Lainzer Tiergarten; adult/under 19yr €5/2.50; ☽ 10am-6pm Tue-Sun late-Mar–Oct; ▯ 60). Franz Josef I commissioned the latter and presented it to his wife as a gift, in an attempt to patch up their failing marriage. Built by Karl von Hasenauer between 1882 and 1886, with Klimt and Makart on board as interior decorators, the villa is suitably plush. Empress Elisabeth's bedroom is an indulgent Shakespearean folly, with the walls and ceilings covered in motifs from A Midsummer Night's Dream. However, for all its opulence and comforts, the villa unfortunately did not have the desired effect: Elisabeth never really took to the place and rarely ventured back to Vienna. She did, however, coin its name, Hermesvilla, after her favourite Greek god.

including giant pandas that arrived in 2003 and a batch of emus, armadillos and baby Siberian tigers that joined them in 2006. Thankfully, most of the original cramped cages have been updated and improved. The zoo's layout is reminiscent of a bicycle wheel, with pathways radiating out from an octagonal pavilion. The pavilion dates from 1759 and was used as the imperial breakfast room. Feeding times are staggered throughout the day – maps on display tell you who's dining when.

🎟 WAGENBURG

☎ 525 24-0; 13, Schloss Schönbrunn; adult/under 19yr €6/free; 🕙 9am-6pm Apr-Oct, 10am-4pm Nov-Mar; 🚇 U4 Schönbrunn 🚃 10A

The Wagenburg (Imperial Coach Collection) is *Pimp My Ride* imperial-style. There is a vast array of carriages on display, including Emperor Franz Stephan's coronation carriage, with its ornate gold plating, Venetian glass panes and painted cherubs. The whole thing weighs an astonishing 4000kg. Also look for the dainty child's carriage built for Napoleon's son, with eagle-wing-shaped mudguards and bee motifs.

🎟 WÜSTENHAUS

☎ 877 92 943 90; 13, Maxingstrasse 13b; adult/under 18yr €4/2.50; 🕙 9am-6pm May-Sep, to 5pm Oct-Apr; 🚇 U4 Hietzing 🚃 10, 58, 60

The small Wüstenhaus (Desert House), near the Palmenhaus, makes good use of the once-disused Sonnenuhrhaus (Sundial House) to re-create arid desert scenes. There are four sections – Northern Africa and the Middle East, Africa, the Americas, and Madagascar – with rare cacti and live desert animals, such as the naked mole from East Africa.

🍴 EAT

🍴 BRANDAUER'S SCHLOSSBRÄU

Beer Garden   €€

☎ 879 59 70; 13, Am Platz 5; mains €6.90-13.90; 🕙 10am-1am; 🚃 58, 60; ❌ Ⓥ

This grand beer hall is set inside one of Vienna's last Biedermeier dance halls (read: palatial and lofty). The former dance floor now houses a circular bar and the velvet-lined stage is part of the dining area. Outside in the courtyard, tables nestled under chestnut trees provide a quieter option during clement weather. Come as much for the traditional Austrian fare as for the extensive beer selection – or indulge in the excellent-value all-you-can-eat lunch buffet (€7.50; Monday to Friday 11.30am to 3pm).

🍴 QUELL *Beisl* €
☎ 893 24 07; 15, Reindorfgasse 19;
🕙 11am-midnight Mon-Fri; 🚌 12A,
57A; 🗶 Ⓥ

With its panelled-wood interior,
wooden chandeliers and ceramic
stoves, Quell looks like it's been
untouched for years – in fact, so
do many of the clientele! But that's
precisely what makes this traditional *Beisl* (small tavern) feel so
real and distinctly Viennese. The
menu is meat heavy, with oodles
of *Schweinskotelett* (pork cutlets)
and schnitzel options, but there's
also s decent number of fish and
vegetarian fare to suit all tastes.

🍸 DRINK
🍸 CAFÉ DOMAYER *Coffee House*
☎ 877 54 650; 13, Dommayergasse 1;
🕙 7am-10pm; 🚋 58, 60

A short hop from the Schloss and
smack in the middle of upmarket
Hietzing, this former ballroom
turned traditional coffee house
is where Johann Strauss Junior
made his 1844 debut. It's a prime
spot to observe both the tuxedoed waiters and the dignified
ladies, who lunch while sipping
a coffee and devouring one of its
signature cakes. Saturdays feature
live piano music between 2pm
and 4pm.

The hilltop Gloriette overlooks the Neptune Fountain in the Schloss Schönbrunn gardens (p118)   RICHARD NEBESKY

Y CAFÉ GLORIETTE *Coffee House*
☎ 879 13 11; 13, Gloriette; ⏰ 9am-1am; Ⓜ U4 Schönbrunn, Hietzing
This cafe occupies the 18th-century Gloriette – a neoclassical construction built to impress Maria Theresia on a hill behind Schloss Schönbrunn. With sweeping views of the Schloss, its magnificent gardens and the districts to the north, Gloriette offers one of the best views in Vienna. And it's a welcome pit stop after the short but sharp climb up the hill.

Y EDLMOSER *Heuriger*
☎ 889 86 80; www.edlmoser.at; 23, Maurer Lange Gasse, Maurer; 🚌 60
Run by a dynamic young winemaker who apprenticed at California's highly respected Ridge Winery, Michael Edlmoser's outward-looking attitude blends with his deep love of Austrian tradition to create what he calls 'cult' wines. Try them in this 400-year-old house where clean lines, modern wood furnishings and a swath of yellow fabric covering a vine-lined garden fuse old and new, just like his wines. It's open from 2.30pm to midnight daily for roughly the last half of each month from April to November.

Y ZAHEL *Heuriger*
☎ 889 13 18; 23, Maurer Hauptplatz 9, Maurer; 🚌 60

One of the oldest *Heurigen* in Vienna, Zahel occupies a 250-year-old farmer's house on Maurer Hauptplatz. The buffet is laden with Viennese and seasonal cuisine, and wine is for sale to take home. It sometimes closes for weeks at a time; if so, head two blocks south to Maurer Lange Gasse, a street lined with oodles of other *Heurigen*, for more options. It's open from 11.30am to midnight daily in the first two weeks of each month.

⭐ PLAY

🟦 BREITENSEER LICHTSPIELE
Cinema
☎ 982 21 73; www.bsl.at.tf, in German; 14, Breitenseer Strasse 21; Ⓜ U3 Hütteldorfer Strasse 🚌 10, 49
Pretend you've hopped back a century at this exceptional art nouveau cinema. Opened in 1909, it is the oldest cinema in Vienna and still retains its original wooden seats and the atmosphere of a bygone era. Films are usually in English with German subtitles; expect many alternative and independent films and the occasional screenings of the classics.

🟦 MARIONETTENTHEATER
Theatre
☎ 817 32 47; www.marionettentheater. at; 13, Schloss Schönbrunn; tickets adult €10-33, child €7-22; ⏰ box office from

Listen to Mozart in the Orangery   KRZYSZTOF DYDYNSKI

are intricate and eye-catching, and it's a fantastic way to enjoy the playful side of Austrian theatre.

⭐ **ORANGERY** *Live Music Venue*
☎ 812 50 04; www.imagevienna.com; 13, Schloss Schönbrunn; tickets €40-96; ⏰ box office 8.30am-7pm; Ⓜ U4 Schönbrunn 🚊 10, 58 🚌 10A
Schönbrunn's former imperial greenhouse is the location for year-round Mozart and Strauss concerts. Performances last around two hours and begin at 8.30pm daily.

⭐ **REIGEN** *Live Music Venue*
☎ 894 00 94; www.reigen.at, in German; 14, Hadikgasse 62; ⏰ 6pm-4am Sep-Jun, from 7pm Jul & Aug; Ⓜ U4 Hietzing 🚌 60
Reigen's tiny stage is the setting for jazz, blues, latin and world music. It is a simple space that also houses rotating painting, sculpture and photography exhibits, so you can groove and peruse art all in one go.

10am performance days; Ⓜ U4 Schönbrunn 🚊 10, 58 🚌 10A
This small theatre in the court wing of Schloss Schönbrunn puts on marionette performances of much-loved productions, such as *The Magic Flute* (2½ hours) and *Aladdin* (1¼ hours). The puppet costumes – all handmade on site –

MOZART IN THE MAKING
Klangforum Wien (☎ 521 670; www.klangforum.at), an ensemble of 24 artists from nine countries, celebrates a unique collaboration between conductors, composers and interpreters who produce a wide range of musical styles, from improv to edgy jazz and classical notes. Many up-and-coming composers are represented (more than 500 new pieces have premiered since its creation in 1985), so don't be surprised if you are wowed with a sneak peak at the next big thing. The Klangforum performs at various venues around the city – check the website for dates and details.

⭐ **U4** *Club*
☎ 817 11 92; www.u4club.at; 12, Schönbrunner Strasse 222; 🕙 8pm-late Mon, from 10pm Tue-Sun; Ⓤ U4 Meidling Hauptstrasse 🚌 10A

U4 was the birthplace of techno clubbing in Vienna way back when, and its longevity is testament to its ability to roll with the times. A fairly young, studenty crowd are its current regulars, and while the music isn't as cutting edge as it used to be, it still manages to please the masses.

SIME/SIMEONE GIOVANNI
Reflect on the glorious baroque folly of Stift Melk (p127)

>THE DANUBE VALLEY

CRUISING, RAILING & RIDING THE DANUBE VALLEY

Cruising down the Danube with a glass of Riesling in one hand and a camera in the other can be the highlight of a trip to the Danube Valley. Fortresses, terraced vineyards, monasteries – you'll glimpse it all.

DDSG Blue Danube (☎ 01-588 800; www.ddsg-blue-danube.at; 02, Handelskai 265; ❤ 9am-6pm Mon-Fri, ticket sales 10am-5pm daily; ❹ U1 Vorgartenstrasse) runs a Sunday service (one-way/return €23/29.50; from Vienna 8.30am, from Dürnstein 4.40pm) between Vienna and Dürnstein (6 hours upstream, 4¼ hours downstream), stopping at Krems at 2pm and returning from Krems at 5pm. Boats leave from near the DDSG office at Quay 5 (Handelskai 265) alongside the Wien/Reichsbrücke. Tickets can also be purchased from the Twin City Liner sales office on Schwedenplatz in Vienna.

Numerous boat companies, including DDSG Blue Danube, operate boats from Krems to Melk (stopping in at Dürnstein and Spitz from April to October). DDSG boats (one-way/return €20/25) leave Krems at 10.15am all seasons, with extra sailings at 1pm and 3.45pm in late April to September. Return sailings leave at 1.50pm the whole season, plus 11am and 4.15pm late April to September. The trip takes three hours upstream, 1¾ hours downstream, and bicycles can be taken on board all boats free of charge.

Alternatively, combine rail and boat. DDSG Blue Danube and the **Österreiche Bundesbahn** (ÖBB, Austrian Federal Railway; www.oebb.at; adult/6-14yr €46.60/23.30) offer combined train-boat-train tickets for one-way train connections to Krems and Melk, and the boat trip in between the two.

Lastly, you can cruise the valley by bicycle. The 38km section of the route between Krems and Melk is easily done one-way in a single day. Hire a bike in Vienna and bring it with you (p160), or pick one up on arrival – most towns have at least one bike-rental shop. Bicycles (day ticket €5) can be taken on trains to and from Vienna. In Krems, **Shell Station Josef Vogl** (☎ 02732-844 24; Steiner Donaulände 17; bicycle per day €24) is convenient for hiring.

MELK

Melk, 35km from Krems, is home to one of the Danube's most popular attractions – **Stift Melk** (Benedictine Abbey of Melk; ☎ 02752-5550; www.stift melk.at; Abt Berthold Dietmayr Strasse 1; adult/student & child/family €7.70/4.50/15.40, incl guided tour €9.50/6.30/19; 🕑 9am-5.30pm May-Sep, to 4.30pm mid-Mar–Apr & Oct-Nov). Perched on a hill, this imposing monastery-fortress provides an excellent view of the surrounding area. It was once the residence of the Babenberg family, but the Benedictine monks transformed it into a monastery in 1089 – it has stayed that way ever since.

The monastery is an example of baroque gone mad, with endless prancing angels and gold twirls. The highlights are the library and the mirror room, both of which have an extra tier painted on the ceiling (by Paul Troger) to give the illusion of greater height. Imperial rooms, where various dignitaries (including Napoleon) stayed, contain museum exhibits. Guided tours of this Benedictine abbey explain its historical importance and are well worth the extra money. Tours are often in English, but phone ahead to make certain.

Also worth a visit, **Schloss Schallaburg** (☎ 02754-6317; www.schallaburg.at; Anzendorf; adult/child €9/3.50, combined ticket incl Stift Melk €15; 🕑 9am-5pm Mon-Fri, to 6pm Sat), 5km south of Melk, is a 16th-century Renaissance palace with magnificent terracotta arches and regular, prestigious temporary exhibitions. The palace also boasts a permanent exhibition of toys through history.

INFORMATION

Location 83km west of Vienna

Getting there Frequent direct trains travel between Wien Westbahnhof in Vienna and Melk; all require a change in Krems (€15.70, 1¼ to 1½ hours). Boats run Sunday morning services run from Vienna between mid-May and mid-September and combination routes with train and boat also exist. See left.

Tourist Office Melk (☎ 02752-523 07-410; www.niederoesterreich.at/melk; Babenbergerstrasse 1; 🕑 9am-noon & 2-6pm Mon-Fri, 10am-noon Sat & Sun May-Aug, 9am-noon Mon-Fri, 10am-2pm Sat Apr, Sep & Oct)

When to go March to November

KREMS

The stretch of the valley between Krems and Melk is known as the Wach-au. This is easily the most spectacular section of the Danube in Austria. Krems (population 24,000), on the northern bank of the Danube, is one of the larger towns in the Wachau region. It's surrounded by terraced vine-yards, has been a centre of the wine trade for most of its history, and to-day it also has a small university. With its historical core (dating back more than 1000 years) and excellent restaurants, it's a perfect starting point for exploring the culinary, vinicultural and historical sights of the Wachau.

The town comprises three parts: Krems, to the east; the smaller settle-ment of Stein, 2km to the west; and the connecting suburb of Und – an unusual name that inspires the joke: 'Krems and (und in German) Stein are three towns'.

The tourist office has an excellent walk-by-numbers map that leads you past the town's sights. The walk begins at the imposing 15th-century **Steiner Tor** (Stein town gate), takes in the **Pfarrkirche St Veit** (☎ 02732-832 85; Pfarrplatz 5; ☀ dawn-dusk), with its colourful 18th-century frescoes, and the **Piaristenkirche** (☎ 02732-820 92; Frauenbergplatz; ☀ dawn-dusk) before taking you to the **Weinstadt Museum** (☎ 02732-801 567; www.weinstadtmuseum.at; Körnermarkt

Stroll the cobblestones in Krems

KRZYSZTOF DYDYNSKI

INFORMATION

Location 64km west of Vienna

Getting there Frequent direct trains travel between Franz-Josefs-Bahnhof in Vienna and Krems (€13.90, one hour). Sunday morning boat services run from Vienna between mid-May and mid-September, and combination routes with train and boat also exist (see p126 for details).

Krems Tourism (☎ 02732-826 76; www.krems.info; Utzstrasse 1; ☾ 9am-6pm Mon-Fri, 11am-5pm Sat, 11am-4pm Sun May-Oct, 9am-5pm Mon-Fri Nov-Apr)

When to go March to November

14; adult/child €4/2; ☾ 10am-6pm Wed-Sat, 1-6pm Sun Mar-Nov), housed in a former Dominican monastery. The museum houses collections of religious and modern art (including works by Kremser Schmidt, who also did the frescoes in Pfarrkirche St Veit) and winemaking artefacts.

Approaching Stein in the west, you reach Krems' **Kunstmeile**, where you can find some first-rate art. The **Kunsthalle** (☎ 02732-908 010-19; www.kunsthalle. at; Franz-Zeller-Platz 3; adult/under 19yr €9/3.50; combined ticket incl 3 Kunstmeile museums €11; ☾ 10am-6pm Apr-Oct, to 5pm Nov-Mar) is small, but has excellent changing exhibitions. Opposite, the **Karikaturmuseum** (☎ 02732-908 020; www.karikaturmuseum. at, in German; Steiner Landstrasse 3a; adult/under 19yr €9/3.50; ☾ 10am-6pm Apr-Oct, to 5pm Nov-Mar) also features changing exhibitions and a large permanent collection of caricatures, including cartoons by Manfred Deix, a legendary Austrian with an eye for the absurd coupled with sharp social commentary.

Make sure you continue to **Schürerplatz** and **Rathausplatz** in Stein, a magnificent part of Krems with the feel of an Adriatic village.

There are numerous *Heurigen* (wine taverns) just out of town. The tourist office has a calendar showing when each is open. **Weingut der Stadt Krems** (☎ 02732-801 441; Stadtgraben 11; ☾ 9am-noon & 1-5pm Mon-Fri, 9am-1pm Sat) is the city-owned vineyard, yielding about 200,000 bottles per year (90% is Grüner Veltliner and Riesling), some of which you can sample free and buy.

For food and drink, sleek student restaurant and bar **Filmbar im Kesselhaus** (☎ 02732-893 3599; www.filmbar.at, in German; Dr-Karl-Dorreck-Strasse 30; mains €5-10, 2-/3-course lunch €6.90/7.90; ☾ 10am-2.30pm Mon & Tue, to midnight Wed-Sun) is the hub of eating and drinking activity on the university campus.

One of the best restaurants in the Wachau is **Mörwald im Kloster Und** (☎ 02732-704 930; Undstrasse 6; 3-course lunch €25, mains €20-33, 5-course menu €85; ☾ 11am-11pm Tue-Sat). It's the most central of a crop of restaurants run by Toni Mörwald outside Vienna, and features exquisite delights ranging from roast pigeon breast to beef, poultry and fish dishes with French angles. A lovely yard and an impressive wine selection round it off.

A crossover crowd of students and mellow jazz types gathers at **Piano** (☎ 02732-858 09; Steiner Landstrasse 21; 🕐 5pm-2am Mon-Thu, to 3am Fri & Sat, to midnight Sun), a lively and off-beat pub that does a couple of local sausage snacks to go with its great selection of beer.

DÜRNSTEIN

The section of the Wachau on the northern bank of the Danube between Krems and the bridge crossing to Melk takes you through Dürnstein. The town achieved 12th-century notoriety for its imprisonment of King Richard the Lionheart of England.

High on the hill, commanding a marvellous view of the curve of the Danube, stand the ruins of **Kuenringerburg**, where Richard was incarcerated from 1192 to 1193. His crime was insulting Leopold V; his misfortune was being recognised despite his disguise when journeying through Austria on his way home from the crusades. His liberty was achieved only upon the payment of a huge ransom, which funded the building of Wiener Neustadt. The hike up from the village takes 15 to 20 minutes.

Anyone wishing to hike further can take the **Schlossbergweg** (marked green) from here to the forest tavern **Fesslhütte** (☎ 02732-41277; www .fesslhuette.at, in German; Dürsteiner Waldhütten 23; goulash €2.30; 🕐 9.30am-6pm Wed-Sun Easter-Oct), about one hour by foot from the castle, to enjoy some sausage, soup or wine. A road also leads up here from Weissenkirchen.

The dominating feature of Dürnstein is the blue spire of the **Chorherren-stift** (Abbey church; ☎ 02711-375; Stiftshof; adult/child €2.60/1.50; 🕐 9am-6pm Apr-Oct). Its

---

INFORMATION

Location 73km west of Vienna

Getting there Frequent direct trains travel between Franz-Josefs-Bahnhof in Vienna and Dürnstein, all require a change in Krems (€15.70, 1¼ to 1½ hours). Sunday morning boat services run from Vienna between mid-May and mid-September, and combination routes with train and boat also exist (see p126 for details).

Tourist Office Dürnstein (☎ 02711-200; www.duernstein.at; Dürnstein Bahnhof; 🕐 9am-2pm Apr–mid-May & early Oct, to 5pm mid-May–Sep).

When to go March to November

Many travellers would pay a king's ransom to get *to* Dürnstein

MARTIN MOOS

baroque interior effectively combines white stucco and dark wood, and its balcony offers a grand view of the Danube.

Travelling west from Dürnstein alongside the Danube, you pass beneath steep hills densely covered with vineyards. Riesling and Grüner Veltliner are grown in these parts, and served in traditional *Heurigen*. Six kilometres on from Dürnstein is **Weissenkirchen**. Its centrepiece is a fortified **parish church** (☎ 02715-2203; Weissenkirchen 3; admission free; ✆ 8am-7pm Easter-Oct, to 5pm Sat & Sun Nov-Easter) rising from a hill, with a labyrinth of covered pathways leading to its front doors. This Gothic church was built in the 15th century and has an impressive baroque altar. Directly below the church is the tiny **Wachau Museum** (☎ 02715-2268; Weissenkirchen 32; adult/child/ concession €5/2.50/3.50; ✆ 10am-5pm Tue-Sun Apr-Oct), which showcases artists of the Danube School.

For a bite, try **Restaurant Loibnerhof** (☎ 02732-828 90-0; Unterloiben 7, Dürnstein-Unterloiben; mains €15-26, 3- & 4-course menu €26-52; ✆ 11.30am-midnight Wed-Sun). Situated 1.5km east of Dürnstein's centre, this family-run restaurant inside a 400-year-old building has a lovely garden where you can enjoy delicious seasonal specialities.

OBST- & GEMÜSE
Slavoljub Milosevic
1020 Wien, Karmelitermarkt 54 - 57   Tel.: 01 / 214

The Viennese match and contradict their stereotypes in one fell swoop. One moment they're donning formal attire to attend a ball or a Mozart concert in a palace, the next they're sipping cocktails in edgy digs wearing retro threads. Snapshots covers it all, from fusion fare gone wild to where to commune with nature.

KRZYSZTOF DYDYNSKI
Cross cultural lines at Karmelitermarkt (p109)

>ACCOMMODATION

From palatial abodes to swanky minimalism, from youth hostels to luxury establishments such as the **Hotel Imperial** (www.luxurycollection.com/imperial) and **Hotel Sacher** (www.sacher.com) – where chandeliers, antique furniture and original 19th-century oil paintings are the norm rather than the exception – Vienna's lodgings cover it all. In the mix are homely *Pensionen* (guesthouses) – which can be far more personable than hotels and less standardised, with larger rooms – and less-ostentatious hotels, plus a small but smart range of apartments. Many of the cheapest older hotels and *Pensionen* rooms share a toilet and shower with other guests.

Standards are high, and so are prices. As a rule, budget doubles are available for under €80 a night, midrange from €80 to €200, and the sky's the limit in this city for top-end accommodation. Breakfast is invariably included in the price – normally a Continental buffet. Peak season is June to September, Christmas and New Year, and Easter.

The central Innere Stadt is the priciest (doubles cost roughly €175 in high season) and most popular area to stay. You can walk to many of the major attractions and the most popular (also the most touristy) restaurants and coffee houses. You'll also find a smattering of nightlife options here. The convenience of this area is undisputed. But do take note that in high summer season its narrow streets are clogged with visitors.

For those seeking both proximity to main sights and nightlife as well as affordability, Neubau, Mariahilf and Wieden are your best bets. You'll never be far from bohemian and trendy bars and excellent restaurants (everything from casual to upscale). This is also home to the foodie destination of choice, the Naschmarkt. Another wallet-friendly option close to the centre is the Josefstadt and Alsergrund area. This is a quieter area with a handful of mainly upmarket restaurants in its core, and the Gürtel bars fill its west-

---

lonely planet Hotels & Hostels

Need a place to stay? Find and book it at lonelyplanet.com. Many Vienna properties are featured – each personally visited, thoroughly reviewed and happily recommended by a Lonely Planet author. From hostels to high-end hotels, we've hunted out the places that will bring you unique and special experiences. Read independent reviews by authors and other travellers, and get practical information including amenities, maps and photos. Then reserve your room simply and securely via Hotels & Hostels – our online booking service. It's all at lonelyplanet.com/hotels.

ern section. Beyond these, Vorstadt Landstrasse (covered in the Belvedere to the Canal chapter) offers little in the way of sights beyond the Belvedere, but is a quiet neighbourhood well connected by tram and subway.

East of the Danube Canal, Leopoldstadt is a top choice. Public transport swiftly whisks you to the main sights, and you're close to up-and-coming bars, restaurants and nightlife. And in the summer, you're only a hop from the Danube and its adjacent green spaces. Schönbrunn and around is residential and light on sights – you'll be close to the palace but little else.

WEB RESOURCES

Despite its name, **Wien Pension** (www.wien-pension.at) specialises in a variety of accommodation options, in all price ranges. **Deutsche Pensionen** (www.deutsche -pensionen.de/oesterreich) is a German site but has a decent Austria section, covering a gamut of *Pensionen* in the capital. **VHO** (www.vho.at) contains a slew of last-minute deals across the budget to midrange category.

IF YOU LOVE...
> Free Sekt (sparkling wine) at breakfast – Hotel Drei Kronen (www.hotel3kronen.at)
> Biedermeier and art nouveau – Hotel am Schubertring (www.schubert ring.at)
> Hangin' with rock bands – Hotel Fürstenhof (www.hotel-fuerstenhof. com)
> Hip design on a budget – All You Need Vienna 2 (www.allyouneed hotels.at)
> Designer digs with a sense of humour – Tyrol (www.das-tyrol.at)
> Upscale apartments – Belvedere Appartements (www.belv.at)

TOP THREE PENSIONS
> Altstadt (www.altstadt.at)
> Pension Hargita (www.hargita.at)
> Schweizer Pension (www.schweizer pension.com)

BEST FOR...
> Simple rooms in a Benedictine monastery – Benediktushaus (www.benediktushaus.at)
> Wine connoisseurs – Hotel Rathaus Wein und Design (www.hotel -rathaus-wien.at)
> Gay Travellers – Pension Wild (www.pension-wild.com)
> Ecofriendly sleeps – Boutiquehotel Stadthalle (www.hotelstadthalle.at)

TOP THREE INNERE STADT STAYS
> Hotel Kärnterhof (www.karntnerhof. com)
> Hollmann Beletage (www.hollmann -beletage.at)
> Aviano (www.secrethomes.at)

>ARCHITECTURE

Due to the Habsburgs' unquestioned desire to clad everything in baroque stylings, little remains of Vienna's art and architectural legacy before the 17th century. Roman ruins are visible at the Römer Museum (p44) in Hoher Markt and the 12th-century Ruprechtskirche (p44), the city's oldest church, which graces the Innere Stadt's old Jewish quarter. And the crowning glory of the Gothic era is the Stephansdom (p46).

Unsurprisingly, it's hard to turn a corner in Central Vienna and its surrounds without running into a baroque wall. Much of the Hofburg (p38) is a baroque showpiece, but it is the highly esteemed Belvedere Palace (Schloss Belvedere; p98) that stands out as one of world's most exquisite examples of baroque architecture. Masterful rococo styling dominates at Schloss Schönbrunn (p117), but the former royal residence is upstaged by its graceful baroque gardens.

Palais Liechtenstein, the former residence of the Liechtenstein family and another gorgeous example of baroque architecture, now houses the Liechtenstein Museum (p74), which contains one of the largest private collections of baroque paintings and sculptures in the world.

The Ringstrasse provides a quick lesson in neoclassicism. High Renaissance can be seen at Gottfried Semper's Naturhistorisches Museum (p42) and Karl von Hasenauer's Kunsthistorisches Museum (p41). Theophil von Hansen designed the Ring's Parlament (p43), one of the last major Greek Revival works built in Europe, while Heinrich von Ferstel's Votivkirche (p75) is a classic example of neo-Gothic. But the showiest building on the Ring, with its dripping spires and spun-sugar facades, is Friedrich von Schmidt's unmissable, Flemish-Gothic Rathaus (p43). The most notable neobaroque example is Eduard van der Nüll's

OTTO WAGNER METRO STATIONS
See our pull-out map for a subway map.
> Stadtplan Pavillions at Karlsplatz (Map p85, E1)
> Nussdorfer Strasse
> Gumpendorfer Strasse
> Ottakring

MOST NOTABLE BUILDINGS
> Belvedere Palace (p98)
> Fernwärme incinerator (p74)
> Hofburg (p38)
> Rathaus (p43)
> Schloss Schönbrunn (p117)
> Stephansdom (p46)

Staatsoper (p55), though it's also worth having a look at Semper's Burgtheater (p53).

Otto Wagner was one of Vienna's most important architects (see the boxed texts, p58 and p151); his most impressive flourishes can be seen at the handful of glorious metro stations he designed (see left). One of the most accessible designs of Adolf Loos is the dim but glowing Loos American Bar (p52), a place of heavy ceilings and boxy booths just off Kärntner Strasse. Also worth a look are his public toilets on the Graben (p38). But the Loos Haus (p41), built between 1909 and 1911, is his most celebrated example.

In terms of modern architecture, Hundertwasser Haus (pictured below; p99) attracts tourists by the bus load, as does the nearby KunstHausWien (p101). However, Friedensreich Hundertwasser's greatest coup is the Fernwärme (p74) incinerator; opened in 1992, it's the most non-industrial-looking heating plant you'll ever see.

Of the 21st-century architectural pieces, the MuseumsQuartier (p56) impresses the most; while the Gasometer (p99) complex is another modern construction to adapt and incorporate historical buildings.

KRZYSZTOF DYDYNSKI

>FOOD

One of the most exciting aspects of visiting Vienna is indulging in the local cuisine, which is currently experiencing a renaissance. It's driven by a new wave of talented Viennese chefs, as well as by a movement back to Vienna's culinary roots – best typified by the *Beisln* (a word of Yiddish origin meaning 'little houses'), the traditional beer houses where enjoying good, homemade-style food is just as important as sipping a fine wine or beer. *Neo-beisln* are a modern take on these classics, where traditional recipes are infused with new culinary takes.

Undoubtedly, the best-known classic Vienna dish is *Wiener Schnitzel*. *Gulasch* (goulash), another dish familiar to almost everyone, arguably attains its highest form as the *Rindsgulasch* (beef goulash). *Tafelspitz* (prime boiled beef) has conquered, if not the world, German speaking countries. It often swims in the juices of the locally produced *Suppengrün* (fresh soup vegetables) it's stewed in, and is served with *Kren* (horseradish) sauce. *Beuschel* (offal; usually sliced lung and heart with a slightly creamy sauce) is another common *Beisln* dish; at Aubergine (p48) it has been elevated to new culinary heights by chef Florian Hrachowina, who adds locally produced snails, topped off by snail caviar.

The undeniable monarchs of all desserts are *Kaiserschmarrn* (sweet pancake with raisins) and *Apfelstrudel* (apple strudel). But also look out for *Marillenknödel* (apricot dumplings), in summer.

The trend in recent years has been towards the *Locovare* (local) and the seasonal, which usually go hand in hand. Vienna feasts from the rural regions in its backyard. The best *Marillen* (apricots) come from the Wachau in the Danube Valley, where about 180 producers harvest around mid-July, throwing Viennese gourmands into a state of *Marille* madness. Marchfeld asparagus, from the southern Weinvertal, reaches Viennese tables from late April, and beef from the Waldviertel (hung for at least 10 days) is served in traditional *Beisln* year-round.

Expect spring lamb in April, *Eierschwammerln* (chanterelle forest mushrooms) in August, and duck and game in September and October respectively, before reaching the culinary highlight of Austria's festive season: goose in November and December.

A key factor to your culinary enjoyment will also be the type of place you choose to eat in. *Kaffeehäuser* (coffee houses; see p16) serve traditional fare of average quality alongside their famed coffees and cakes. *Beisln* (p18) are a must-do and offer the most traditional fare, while

Heurigen (wine taverns; p14), mostly on the outskirts of the city, sport overflowing buffets of salads and pork, plus an endless supply of new wine. In keeping with the Habsburg tradition, if a restaurant has a French influence, it will invariably be more expensive.

BEST TRADITIONAL BEISLN

> Beim Czaak (p48)
> Gasthaus Wickerl (p76)
> Zu den 2 Lieserln (p65)

BEST FOR

> Cured ham: Silberwirt (p91)
> Naschmarkt culinary bliss: Neni (pictured below; p91)
> Chic Vienna meets the Med: Aubergine (p48)

KRZYSZTOF DYDYNSKI

>DRINKING

Kicking back with a glass of wine or beer or turning back time with coffee in an ancient *Kaffeehäuser* while engaging in a heated discussion or simply having a laugh – it all has a special place in the hearts and minds of the Viennese.

Drinking is a big part of the cultural make-up of the city. Despite the Viennese love for heading out on the town for quality cocktails, they never forget they live in the coffee capital of the world. The city's *Kaffeehäuser* are as famous as the city's classical-music heritage, and an attraction in their own right (see p16). The sheer number of *Kaffeehäuser* is staggering, but each has its own flair and flavour.

Ordering with 'a coffee, please' won't go down well in most coffee houses. A quick glance at a menu will uncover an unfathomable list of coffee choices, including plenty with a shot of alcohol. Some of the most popular options include *Brauner* (black, but served with a tiny splash of milk), *Verlängerter* (*Brauner* weakened with hot water), *Fiaker* (*Verlängerter* with rum and whipped cream), *Melange* (the Viennese classic, served with milk, and maybe whipped cream, similar to a cappuccino). *Wiener Eiskaffee* (cold coffee with vanilla ice cream and whipped cream) is a sound choice during Vienna's steamy summers. And most styles come in *Gross* (large) or *Klein* (small). Whatever you order, a good coffee house will serve your cup on a silver platter accompanied by a glass of water and a small sweet.

In terms of alcoholic drinks, wine is most beloved by the Viennese. Seven sq km of vineyards lie within Vienna's borders, making it the world's largest wine-growing city. *Heurigen* (see p14), the city's equivalent of a wine tavern, are rustic establishments on the outskirts of the city where 'new' wine (normally only a year old) is served to eager patrons on warm summer evenings.

Vienna also has a kicking bar scene. Many locations feature DJs on a regular basis and begin to fill from around 8pm or 9pm. The scene is highly accommodating to all tastes, ages and moods: from grunged-up student hang-outs to sophisticated wine or cocktail bars and everything in between. The distinction between bar and restaurant, club or coffee house is often blurred.

Concentrations of bars and are spread throughout the city. While the Innere Stadt never seems to empty of people, its scene is small and limited to a few select bars. The Bermuda Dreieck (Bermuda Triangle) in the old Jewish Quarter is rammed with places, but most are heavily touristy or not worth your time. East of the Danube Canal, Leopoldstadt (see p104) is the new darling of Vienna's night owls; its bars and clubs ooze 'underground' and attract a motley crew of students and artists. Collectively, the Naschmarkt and the rest of Wieden (p84) and Mariahilf (p56) contain the largest consolidation of bars. Schleifmühlgasse (see Map p85, D2), and Gumpendorfer Strasse (see Map p57, E3) in particular, has some good pickings, as does most of Neubau (p56). Around Josefstädter and Nussdorfer Strasse U-Bahn station on the Gürtel is yet another area sporting a profusion of bars – many under the *Stadtbogen* (arched spaces below the U-Bahn line), some of which are leaders in the electronica and live-music scene, others of which have gone glam.

KRZYSZTOF DYDYNSKI

BEST FOR...
> Creative cocktails: Halbestadt (p79)
> Architectural accompaniment for your cocktails: Loos American Bar (p52)

BEST KAFFEEHÄUSER FOR...
> Hip atmosphere: Café Drechsler (pictured above; p65)
> Traditional vibes: Café Sperl (p66)
> The famous *Torte*: Café Sacher (p52)

BEST HEURIGEN & STADTHEURIGEN
> Edlmoser (p122)
> Weinstube Josefstadt (p81)
> Mayer am Pfarrplatz (p80)

BEST FOR SAMPLING AUSTRIAN WINE
> Vis-a-Vis (p53)
> Wein & Wasser (p81)
> Sekt Comptoir (p94)
> Joanelli (p67)

>OPERA & CLASSICAL MUSIC

Vienna is the world capital of opera and classical music. Who else can claim Mozart, Beethoven, Strauss and Schubert among its historical repertoire? The rich musical legacy that flows through the city is evident everywhere. There are a plethora of monuments around the city to its greatest composers, and its princely music venues easily outnumber those of some whole countries, let alone other capital cities.

And it doesn't end there. You can listen to Mozart in a space where he once practised, such as Schloss Schönbrunn's Orangery (p123); embrace decadence and operatic masterpieces at one of the finest opera houses in Europe, the Staatsoper (p55); be wowed by the sights and sounds of the world-renowned Vienna Philharmonic; and sway to the chorus of unceasing classical-music concerts at a whole array of fabulous venues.

Vienna's churches and *Kaffeehäuser* also make fine venues to enjoy classical music. Augustinerkirche (p35) and Burgkapelle (p38) are just some of the city's churches that complement Sunday morning Mass with a full choir and orchestra; some also have regular evening concerts. A handful of *Kaffeehäuser* also feature regular classical-music performances. It's a distinctly Viennese way to while away an afternoon or evening, and only costs the price of a cup of coffee (though we dare you to resist a slice of something sweet from the pastry case). For the full list of where to hear what, pick up the handy *Wiener Konzert Cafés* (Vienna's Concert Cafes) brochure from the tourist office.

GREG ELMS

BEST FOR...
> Classical at a cafe: Café Prückel (p50)
> The Philharmonic: Musikverein (p54)
> Opera: Staatsoper (pictured right; p55)

BEST FOR STRAUSS & MOZART
> Kursalon (p54)
> Hofburg Concert Halls (p53)
> Wiener Residenzorchester at the Auersperg palace (p83)
> Orangery (p123)

>GAY & LESBIAN

Vienna is fairly tolerant towards gays and lesbians, and things are getting better each year. Even the Vienna Tourist Board does their bit; their *Queer Guide* booklet has listings of bars, restaurants, hotels and festivals, while their *Vienna Gay Guide* is a city map with gay locations marked on it. *Xtra* and *Night Life* (www.nightlifeonline.at, in German), two free monthly publications, are additional supplements packed with news, views and listings (in German only). Rainbow (www.rainbow.at/guide) also has a scene guide for Vienna.

Gay and lesbian travellers should beeline to the **Rosa Lila Villa** (off Map p57, D4; ☎ 586 81 50; www.villa.at; 06, Linke Wienzeile 102), the best organisation in town. It's housed in an unmissable pink house by the Wien River and contains a cafe, **Lesbian Centre** (☎ 586 81 50; ⌚ 5-8pm Mon, Wed & Fri) and **Gay Men's Centre** (☎ 585 43 43; ⌚ 5-8pm Mon, Wed & Sat). **Homosexualle Initiative Wien** (Map p106, C5; ☎ 216 66 04; www.hosiwien.at, in German; 02, Novaragasse 40) is another helpful organisation and is politically minded. All of the above offer extensive local information about the gay and lesbian scene and hold regular events.

Vienna has enough bars and clubs to entertain its gay and lesbian community, while some straight clubs, such as U4 (p124), feature gay nights on a weekly basis. Some popular hang-outs include part-bookshop, part-cafe Café Berg (pictured below; p79); the women-only Frauencafé (p79); and trendy cocktail-bar and nightlife-haunt Mango Bar (p68). There are also a number of gay and lesbian bars clustered around the Rosa Lila Villa.

© YADID LEVY / ALAMY

>SHOPPING

Don't even think about visiting Vienna without hitting the shops. The boutique scene – particularly along Kirchengasse, Neubaugasse and Lindengasse in Neubau (see Map p57, D2, C3 and D3) – is exploding with young designers' spaces selling quality affordable creations you'll never see on someone else. For a partial list of shops, check out www.7tm.at. Neubau's northern edge also brims with the city's idiosyncratic *Altwaren* (old wares) shops (rummaging through secondhand treasures and trash is de rigueur) and *Jugendstil* (art nouveau) showrooms filled with both furniture and jewellery. But in this market, the famous *Flohmarkt* (flea market; see p86) adjacent to Naschmarkt reigns supreme.

Another quintessentially Viennese shopping experience is bidding on authentic antique furniture, jewellery and art at famed local auction house Dorotheum (see the boxed text, p48). For excellent gallery-hopping or shopping for period and contemporary art, antique guns, porcelain and armour, hit the streets between the Dorotheum and Albertinaplatz (see Map p36, D5). Additionally, you can buy Viennese sweets to eat or send home – cafes such as the Café Sacher (p52) and Aida (p50) offer boxed cakes to take home, and Sacher even ships its famous *Torte* worldwide.

In the tiny Innere Stadt, the area around Hoher Markt (see Map p37, E2) brims with fashion and small boutiques, many selling locally designed clothes and accessories. Outside the Ring, your best bets for a pleasant afternoon's shopping are Mariahilf and Neubau (see Map p57, D2 and F3), where you'll find plenty of quirky one-offs and interesting boutiques. For more details on the shopping scene, see p62.

BEST FOR

> Sustainable style: gabarage upcycling design (p88)
> Local designer clothing: The Hot Dogs (p63)
> Jam: Stauds (p77)
> Art deco and Bauhaus furniture: Holzer Galerie (p60)
> Extravagant cakes: Aida (p50)

MADE IN VIENNA

> Art Up (p46)
> Vienna Bag (p48)
> Wiener Porzellanmanufaktur Augarten (p110)
> Wie Wien (p88)
> Perzy Snow Globes (p82)

>OUTDOOR VIENNA

Being active and outdoors is in the Viennese blood, despite all the cigarettes they smoke. With much of the country given over to mountainous splendour, snow sports are hugely popular in Austria. The best skiing is in the western reaches of the country, but Greater Vienna even has a couple of tiny slopes in its hills.

Hiking in the immediate area around Vienna is a breeze – hop on a tram or a bus to an end stop, and start climbing. Some of the most accessible places to embark on a hike are the Wienerwald (Vienna Woods) and the Lainzer Tiergarten (see p119) on the city's western fringes. Many of the routes are suited for casual hikers, and the beauty of it all is that you'll likely also stumble across a *Heuriger* or three, a perfectly respectable way to end a day of walking. Beyond the immediate city limits, the towns of the Danube Valley also make excellent bases for walking (see p126 for details).

The old and new waterways of the Danube are literally made for swimming and boating. Green parklands such as the Prater (p104) and Donauinsel (Danube Island; p113) provide plenty of space to stretch the legs, walk and tool through on a bike. In fact, cycling is one of the best ways to enjoy the outdoors and see the city (see p160 for info on where to hire a bike).

After all that outdoor activity, you might be tempted to hit a *hammam* (Turkish steam bath). The city's best is located inside a space that doubles as a club (Aux Gazelles; p69).

Vienna and its outskirts provide plenty of green spaces for outdoor enthusiasts

RICHARD NEBESKY

>AFTER DARK

Vienna's electronic scene is in the midst of a revival. DJ Glow is known for his electro beats; legends Kruder & Dorfmeister live and work in Vienna; the Sofa Surfers serve up often-dark but well-received dub-hop tracks; and international DJs spin the latest beats at the 1950s sauna-turned-club Pratersauna (p113), where light installations pulsate next to dancing masses.

Most local folk detest queuing and hefty entry prices, so clubs are generally quite intimate. The dividing line between a club and bar is often quite blurred and hard to pick. Most contemporary bars feature DJs on a regular basis and some, such as Europa (p67), Tanzcafé Jenseits (p69), Café Leopold (p66) and Wirr (p69) have small but well-used dance floors. Legendary U4 (p124) has been thumping for more than 30 years and once hosted Nirvana and Falco – but these days it's best known for its theme nights, from disco to hard rock.

The Gürtel clubs – venues wedged under the elevated subway tracks in Josefstadt and Alsergrund – are hopping most nights of the week. Late August brings the annual **Gürtel Night Walk** (www.guertelnightwalk.at) when the action spills out to the pavements lining the Gürtel, with international acts performing on open-air stages. The reinvention of the Danube Canal as a bar strip has seen growth, with several nightspots scattered along its shores.

Formerly the end of the line for bands touring Europe, Vienna is now a crossroads for those heading to Eastern Europe. Big-name and new bands regularly perform on the city's stages, such as the **Stadthalle** (www.stadthalle.com) and **Szene Wien** (www.szenewien.com). The yearly repertoire is a healthy mix of jazz, rock (both alternative and mainstream) and world music. Bars and clubs, in particular **Flex** (www.flex.at, in German), Rhiz (p80) and Chelsea (p79), regularly host touring bands.

Pore over Carl Kundmann's Athena Fountain (p43)

DAVID RYAN

HISTORY

Situated at a natural crossing of the Danube (Donau) River, Vienna was probably an important trading post for the Celts when the Romans arrived around 15 BC. The Roman settlement – called Vindobona, after the Celtic tribe Vinid – blossomed into a town by the 3rd and 4th centuries AD, and vineyards were introduced to the surrounding area. The forerunner of the city's modern name – Wenia – first surfaced in official documents in 881.

Over the ensuing centuries, control of Vienna changed hands a number of times, until the Babenbergs came to power and formed a dynasty that ruled for 270 years – until 1246, when Duke Friedrich II died in battle, leaving no heirs. This allowed the ambitious Bohemian king, Ottokar II, to move in and take control. He bolstered his claim to Austria by marrying Friedrich II's widow.

Ottokar gained support from Vienna's burghers by founding a hospital for the poor and rebuilding Stephansdom after a destructive fire in 1258. However, he refused to swear allegiance to the new Holy Roman Emperor, Rudolf von Habsburg, and his pride proved costly – Ottokar died in a battle against his powerful adversary at Marchfeld in 1278. Rudolf's success on the battlefield began the rule of one of the most powerful dynasties in history, a dynasty that would retain power right up to the 20th century.

Vienna was a hot bed of revolt and religious bickering during Europe's Reformation and Counter-Reformation, and suffered terribly through plague and siege at the end of the 17th century. The beginning of the 18th century, however, heralded a golden age for Vienna, with baroque architecture, civil reform and a classical-music revolution.

The French Revolution of 1789–99 ushered in a new age of republicanism in Europe, and challenged surviving feudalistic anachronisms such as the Holy Roman Empire. Things turned sour for Vienna at the beginning of the 19th century – Napoleon occupied the city twice, in 1805 and 1809.

Napoleon's reign was brief, but his advance across Europe caused the Holy Roman Empire's collapse. The Habsburgs survived, however, and in the following years, they dominated a loose *Deutscher Bund* (German Alliance) comprising hundreds of small 'states' cobbled together. This was a period of cultural flourishing and was known as the Biedermeier period.

Ordinary citizens at this time, tired of being kept on a short leash by their political masters, also began to seek new freedoms. In 1848, inspired by the revolution in France early that year, Austrians demanded their own parliament. One was created and met in July that year, but revolution and a democratic parliament failed to endure in Austria.

In 1867 a dual monarchy was created in Austria and Hungary. This was an attempt by the Habsburgs to hold onto Hungarian support for the monarchy by giving them a degree of autonomy. This Austro-Hungarian Empire would become known as the KuK (König und Kaiser; King and Kaiser) monarchy – the kaiser of Austria was also king of Hungary.

The advent of WWI stalled Vienna's architectural and cultural development. The Republic of Austria was created on 12 November 1918, and the monarchy was consigned to the past.

The 1920s saw the rise of fascism, and by 1934 civil war broke out in the city streets. The socialists were defeated and Vienna's city council dissolved. Austria was ripe for the picking, when Hitler came along on 15 March 1938. He entered the city to the cheers of 200,000 ecstatic Viennese.

Vienna suffered heavily under Allied bombing in WWII, and on 11 April 1945 advancing Russian troops liberated Vienna (soon after to be joined by the Americans, British and French in Allied occupation); raping and pillaging by the Red Army further scarred an already shattered populace. Soon after liberation Austria declared its independence from Germany and a provisional federal government was established under socialist

DOS & DON'TS: VIENNESE ETIQUETTE

Stick to the following dos and don'ts and you'll do just fine mixing with the Viennese:

> Do greet people with *Grüss Gott* or *Guten Tag*, everywhere from social settings to shops, cafes, restaurants and information offices. *Servus* is reserved for greetings only between friends or the younger generation. When departing, *Auf Wiedersehen* or *Auf Wiederschauen* is appropriate.

> Do shake hands when introduced to someone, even in younger, informal company. Likewise, shake hands when you leave.

> Do dress up if going to the opera, theatre or a top restaurant. A jacket and tie for men is the norm.

> Do use full titles at the beginning of formal meetings: *Herr* for men and *Frau* for women is the minimum required. If you speak German, always use the *Sie* form with the older generation and on the telephone; it's not so common with the younger generation.

> Don't cross at the traffic lights when the figure is red, even when there is no traffic in sight. Viennese rarely do it, and you can be fined on the spot for jaywalking.

Karl Renner. Vienna was divided into four zones; this was the time of 'four men in a jeep', so aptly depicted in Graham Greene's *The Third Man*.

Delays caused by frosting relations between the superpowers ensured that the Allied occupation dragged on for 10 years. It was a tough time for the Viennese – the rebuilding of national monuments was slow and expensive, and the black market dominated the flow of goods. On 15 May 1955 the Austrian State Treaty was ratified, with Austria proclaiming its permanent neutrality. The Allied forces withdrew, and in December 1955 Austria joined the UN. The economy took a turn for the better through the assistance granted under the Marshall Plan, and the cessation of the removal of industrial property by the Soviets. As the capital of a neutral country on the edge of the Cold War front line, Vienna attracted spies and diplomats: Kennedy and Khrushchev met here in 1961, Carter and Brezhnev in 1979; the UN set up shop in 1983.

In a referendum in June 1994 a resounding 66.4% of the populace voted in favour of EU membership, and Austria entered into the EU in 1995. Support soon waned as prices increased with the introduction of the euro, but most Austrians have resigned themselves to the fact that the EU is here to stay.

The impact of the global financial crisis caused a dip in Vienna's tourism and an increase in unemployment, but overall it has weathered the storm fairly well. Clearly, the amount of construction around the new train station development demonstrates the city is looking to the future.

LIFE AS A VIENNESE

Trying to put a finger on the psyche of a capital whose country gave us the psychoanalyst Sigmund Freud is surely fraught with danger. As Freud himself said, 'I know only one thing for sure. The value judgements of human beings are…an attempt to prop up illusion with argument'. So what was he trying to tell us? Maybe that whatever we think about Austrians after visiting Vienna, some of it will be our own narrative.

Even Freud, though, couldn't deny a few things about the Austrians' mental topography. One is the self-styled conservatism you find in the deeper rifts and valleys of its regions. Another is that there are a few historical grains that irritate the Austrian psyche. Once upon a time half the world was its oyster. Now it isn't. But what Austria now lacks in influence it makes up for with a grandiose bureaucracy, honed with vigour since the 19th century. Austrians see themselves – probably quite rightly – as more harmony seeking than their German neighbours, but they can also be greater sticklers for convention. Public opinion is less fragmented, although this has much to do with the country's size.

Austrians are strikingly 'New World' at times, while also fiercely regional. Along with the national symbols, each state has its own anthem, which is sung by school children on important occasions; and each even has its own patron saint.

The Viennese are different in this respect, because they see themselves first and foremost as Austrians. But still, city attitudes prevail. The capital lives and thrives on its *Wiener Schmäh* (Vienna humour), a concoction of morbid, wry, misanthropic wit, as illustrated in some of the local Viennese Actionism art (see the boxed text, p59). Maybe this is why one of Freud's most important works is his *Jokes and their Relation to the Unconscious*. The analysis is all very serious stuff, of course, but the book also happens to be a fine collection of *Schmäh*.

The standard of living remains high here. With a spectacular landscape on its doorstep lending itself to skiing, hiking and extreme sports, and an exciting cultural life, Vienna boasts a quality of life that often sees it

OTTO WAGNER

Otto Wagner (1841–1918) was one of the most influential Viennese architects at the end of the 19th century (the era of fin de siècle). He was trained in the classical tradition, and became a professor at the Akademie der bildenden Künste (Academy of Fine Arts). His early work was in keeping with his education, and he was responsible for some neo-Renaissance buildings along the Ringstrasse. But as the 20th century dawned he developed an art nouveau style, with flowing lines and decorative motifs. Wagner left the Academy to join the looser, more creative Secession movement in 1899 and attracted public criticism in the process – which is one of the reasons his creative designs for Vienna's Historical Museum were never adopted. In the 20th century, Wagner began to strip away the more decorative aspects of his designs, concentrating instead on presenting the functional features of buildings in a creative way.

The most accessible of Wagner's works are his metro stations, scattered along the network (see the boxed text, p136). The metro project, which lasted from 1894 to 1901, included 35 stations, as well as bridges and viaducts. Wagner's stations were designed to blend in with the surrounding architecture, wherever they were built. All of them, however, feature green-painted iron, some neoclassical touches (such as columns), and curvy, all-capitals fin-de-siècle fonts. The earlier stations show the cleaner lines of neoclassicism, while Karlsplatz, built in 1898, is a curvy, exuberant work of Secessionist gilding and luminous glass.

ranked as the most liveable city in the world. Life here brings the excitement and perks of a big city at a pace that is more relaxed than in most other European capitals. This shows in the favoured Viennese pastime of enjoying a beer, wine or coffee with friends in one of the capital's many bars, restaurants or coffee houses. Vienna is also a magnet for artists, students and professionals from all over Austria, who arrive to study, live and work, and often never leave.

ARTS & ARCHITECTURE

In many ways, Vienna's art and architecture have waltzed arm in arm through the ballrooms of history. From its early Roman beginnings to its 21st-century contemporary constructions, the city's good burghers have played with brick and mortar, often mastering, sometimes excelling, in their attempts. In addition to its Renaissance examples, the city is embellished with a healthy array of architectural styles, many of which are evidenced within easy reach of the Innere Stadt. Highlights abound, but the peak periods of baroque and *Jugendstil* (art nouveau) emblazoned the city with a plethora of masterpieces, from greats such as Otto Wagner, that are in a class of their own; for some, their collective brilliance outshines all other attractions in Vienna.

GUSTAV KLIMT & VIENNESE SECESSIONISM

Anthony Haywood

Now usually associated with art nouveau, the Viennese Secession movement was formed by 19 artists in the 1890s in order to break away from the historical or revivalist styles that dominated Europe at the time. The painter Gustav Klimt (1862–1918) was its first president, and other Secession artists included architect Otto Wagner (1841–1918), interior designer and painter Carl Moll (1861–1945) and painter Kolo Moser (1868–1918).

Secession artists worked in a highly decorative style. Klimt's famous painting *The Kiss* (1908) is typical of the rich ornamentation, vivid colour and floral motifs favoured by the movement. His later pictures (such as the two portraits of Adele Bloch-Bauer from 1907) employ a harmonious but ostentatious use of background colour, with much metallic gold and silver to evoke or symbolise the emotion.

Otto Wagner, by contrast, began working in historicist styles (some neo-Renaissance buildings on Vienna's Ringstrasse are by his hand), joined the Secessionists, and with Klimt and others split from them and adopted his own more functional style.

The city's art also peaked in its fin-de-siècle years, spawning *Jugendstil,* the Secession (see left), the *Wiener Werkstätte* (WW; Vienna Workshop) and greats such as Gustav Klimt (see left) and Egon Schiele. The history of WWII and Austria's voluntary embrace of Nazism have created another artistic generation altogether, one that is attempting to come to grips with this unsettling heritage. Perhaps the most vivid expressionism to rise from this group is that of the Viennese Actionism art movement (see p59), whose work revolves around violent self-hatred.

Guilt, self-loathing, a pathological distaste for being Austrian and a fondness for dogs are themes you'll see again and again in Viennese

WHO'S WHO OF VIENNESE COMPOSERS

> **Josef Haydn** People in the know think Haydn (1732–1809) is one of the three greatest classical composers. His greatest works include *Symphony No 102 in B-flat Major,* the oratorios *The Creation* (1798) and *The Seasons* (1801), and six Masses written for Miklós II.

> **Wolfgang Amadeus Mozart** See p17.

> **Ludwig van Beethoven** Beethoven (1770–1827) studied briefly with Mozart in Vienna in 1787; he returned in late 1792. Beethoven produced a lot of chamber music up to the age of 32, when he became almost totally deaf and – ironically – began writing some of his best works, including *Symphony No 9 in D Minor, Symphony No 5* and his late string quartets.

> **Franz Schubert** Born and bred in the city, Schubert (1797–1828) really knew how to churn out a tune: he composed nine symphonies, 11 overtures, seven Masses, over 80 smaller choral works, over 30 chamber-music pieces, 450 piano pieces and over 600 songs – that's more than 960 works in total – before dying of exhaustion at 31. His best-known works are his last symphony *(Great C Major Symphony)*, his Mass in E-flat and the *Unfinished Symphony*.

> **Johann Strauss the Elder & the Younger** The early masters of the waltz, which first became popular at the Congress of Vienna (1814–15), were Johann Strauss the Elder (1804–49) and Josef Lanner (1801–43). Johann Strauss the Younger (1825–99) composed over 400 waltzes, including Vienna's unofficial anthem, 'The Blue Danube' (1867), and 'Tales from the Vienna Woods' (1868). Strauss the Younger also excelled at operettas; his *Die Fledermaus* (The Bat; 1874) and *The Gypsy Baron* (1885) are eternally popular.

> **Johannes Brahms** At the age of 29, Brahms (1833–97) moved to Vienna, where many of his works were performed by the Vienna Philharmonic. His best works include *Ein Deutsches Requiem,* his *Violin Concerto* and *Symphony Nos 1* to *4.*

> **Gustav Mahler** Known mainly for his nine symphonies, German-born Mahler (1860–1911) was director of the Vienna State Opera from 1897 to 1907. His best works include *Das Lied von der Erde* (The Song of the Earth) and *Symphony Nos 1, 5* and *9.*

literature and painting (as well as its cinema). The legacy of WWII is particularly prevalent in the general hatred of humanity demonstrated in author Elfriede Jelinek's novels (p156).

While the Viennese love their contemporary visual arts, visitors are more likely to encounter Viennese music. Contemporary pickings are slim (legendary DJ-duo Kruder & Dorfmeister are definitely the cream of the crop, while nobody can forget Falco's 'Rock Me, Amadeus'), but Vienna's musical history is rich, glorious and immensely accessible. Beethoven, Mozart, Haydn and the Strauss family all did stints in the city, and Vienna isn't about to let you forget it.

CINEMA

Modern Viennese cinema can seem to be a bleak landscape of corrupt and venal characters beating their children and dogs while struggling with a legacy of hatred and guilt. That's a slight exaggeration, but contemporary film does tend to favour naturalism over escapism, violent sex over flowery romance, and ambivalence and dislocation over happy endings where all the threads are tied.

The film industry is lively and productive, turning out Cannes-sweepers including Michael Haneke, of *The Piano Teacher* fame, and festival darlings such as Jessica Hausner, director of the confronting *Lovely Rita*. A healthy serving of government arts funding certainly helps, as does the Viennese passion for a trip to the *Kino* (cinema). Local, independent films are as well attended as blockbusters by Graz-boy-made-good Arnie Schwarzenegger. A yearly festival, Viennale draws experimental and fringe films from all over Europe and keeps the creative juices flowing.

THE VIENNALE

Vienna's annual international film festival, the Viennale, is the highlight of the city's celluloid calendar. By no means as prestigious as Cannes or Berlin, it still attracts top-quality films from all over the world and is geared to the viewer rather than the film-makers. For two weeks from mid-October, city cinemas continuously play screenings that could broadly be described as fringe, ranging from documentaries to short and feature films. Tickets for the more popular screenings and most evening screenings can be hard to come by. Tickets can be purchased two weeks before the festival starts from a number of stands around town. To get a jump on fellow festival-goers, call ☎ 526 59 47 or check www.viennale.at.

THE THIRD MAN & VIENNA

Shot in Vienna in 1948, iconic film *The Third Man* perfectly captures the atmosphere of post-war Vienna, using an excellent play of shadow and light. The plot is simple but gripping. Holly Martin (played by Joseph Cotton), an out-of-work writer, travels to Vienna at the request of his old school mate, Harry Lime (played by Orson Welles), only to find him dead under mysterious circumstances. Doubts over the death drag Martin into the black-market penicillin racket and the path of the multinational force controlling Vienna. Their cat-and-mouse chase across the rubble-filled capital is both haunting and moody, with superb dialogue, a scintillating confrontation aboard the Riesenrad (giant Ferris wheel) and glimpses of Vienna's most recognised landmarks.

The film was an instant success, and has aged with grace and style. It won first prize at Cannes in 1949, the Oscar for Best Camera for a Black and White Movie in 1950, and was selected by the British Film Institute as 'favourite British film of the 20th century' in 1999.

While in town, get your fix at the **Burg Kino** (p53), which screens the film on a weekly basis, or visit the **Third Man Private Collection** (p86). True film aficionados may want to take the detailed guided tour run by **Vienna Walks** (p163).

Meanwhile, art-house cinemas such as the gorgeous *Jugendstil* Breitenseer Lichtspiele (p122) keep the Viennese proud of their rich cinematic history. And Vienna itself has been the star of movies such as *The Third Man* (above), *The Night Porter* and *Before Sunrise*.

These days, Haneke is the big name. His films tend to feature large doses of sadism and masochism. *The Piano Teacher*, based on the novel by Viennese writer Jelinek, won three awards at Cannes in 2001. Another of his films, *The White Ribbon*, a dark tale about a family in Germany shortly before WWI, won the Palme d'Or in 2009 (Cannes' highest prize) and was nominated for two Academy Awards.

Hausner has also made several short films and released her first feature, *Lovely Rita* (the story of a suburban girl who kills her parents in cold blood), in 2001. Her most recent film, *Lourdes* (a story about a wheelchair-bound woman who makes a pilgrimage to Lourdes and finds that she can suddenly walk), received the prize for best film at the 2009 Viennale.

Another prominent figure is documentary-maker Ulrich Seidl, who made *Jesus, You Know*, following six Viennese Catholics as they visit their church for prayer, and *Animal Love,* an investigation of Viennese suburbanites who have abandoned human company for that of pets. In 2001 he branched into features with *Dog Days;* his latest, *Import Export*, was nominated at Cannes in 2007.

Recently, Austria has been celebrating Viennese born actor Christoph Waltz. Waltz, a virtual unknown outside Austria and Germany until he was cast in Quentin Tarantino's *Inglourious Basterds,* shot to international fame for his portrayal of the film's pivotal character, SS Colonel Hans Landa. The role won him the 2010 Academy Award for Best Supporting Actor.

FURTHER READING

The Radetzky March (Joseph Roth, 1932) A study of one family affected by the end of an empire, the themes of *The Radetzky March* are applicable to any society emerging from a long-hated, but at least understood, regime. In some ways, it is about life after God.

The Third Man (Graham Greene, 1950) Put some time aside to read the book Greene designed as a screenplay. There is a lot of intriguing and easily missed detail in this complex story of death, morality and the black market in the rubble of postwar Vienna.

Across (Peter Handke, 1986) Another cheery Viennese novel, *Across* follows an observer of life drawn into 'real being' after he whimsically murders someone. Pretty darn postmodern.

The Devil in Vienna (Doris Orgel, 1978) A book for older kids, *The Devil in Vienna* is the story of two blood-sisters in 1938 Vienna – one Jewish, the other from a Nazi family – and their attempts to maintain their friendship. May get kids all riled up, in a 'why is the world so unjust?' way.

Greed (Elfriede Jelinek, 2006) She's a witty and clever writer, but Jelinek hates all her characters and has a long-standing love/hate relationship with Austria. *Greed* tells the story of a debt-ridden country policeman, his relationships with the townspeople and the lonely local women he manipulates.

>DIRECTORY
TRANSPORT
ARRIVAL & DEPARTURE
AIR
Vienna International Airport

Vienna International Airport (☎ 700 7222 33; www.viennaairport.com) is 20km southwest of the city centre. Facilities include banks and ATMs, money-exchange counters, a supermarket, a post office, car rental agencies and a 24-hour left-luggage counter.

Airport Letisko Bratislava

Bratislava, Slovakia's capital, only 60km east of Vienna, is a highly feasible alternative to flying directly into Austria. **Airport Letisko Bratislava** (☎ 0421 2 4857 3353; www.airportbratislava.sk) is connected to Vienna's International Airport by a **bus** (www.terravision.eu; one way/return €10/16) that runs seven times daily.

TRAIN

Vienna is one of central Europe's main rail hubs. **Österreiche Bundesbahn** (ÖBB, Austrian Federal Railway; ☎ 05 17 17; www.oebb.at) is the main operator. There are direct services and connections to many European cities. Sample train times include Berlin (nine to 10 hours), Budapest (2¾ to four hours), Munich (four to five hours), Paris (12 to 13 hours), Prague (4½ to 5½ hours) and Venice (eight to nine hours).

TRAVEL TO/FROM THE AIRPORT

Bus Link (☎ 32 300; www.postbus.at; one way adult/under 6yr/6-15yr €6/free/3, return €11/free/5.50; ⏱ every 30min from Westbahnhof 5am-11pm, from Meidling 5.15am-11.15pm, from Schwedenplatz 5am-11.30pm, from UNO City 6.38am-6.38pm) The Westbahnhof service calls in at Wien Meidling station.

C&K Airport Service (☎ 444 44; www.ck-airportservice.at; one-way up to 4 passengers €33) C&K car service is a better, cheaper option than a taxi, as its rates are fixed. On arrival at the airport, head to its stand to the left of the exit hall; when leaving Vienna, call ahead to make a reservation.

City Airport Train (CAT; ☎ 252 50; www.cityairporttrain.com; return adult/under 15yr €18/free, booked online €16/free; ⏱ every 30min 5.38am-11.08pm) Departs from Wien Mitte; also offers luggage check-in facilities and boarding-card issuing service.

Schnellbahn 7 (☎ 05 17 17; www.oebb.at; one-way €3.60; ⏱ every 30min 4.32am-9.56pm Mon-Sat) The cheapest way to get to the airport, this train departs from Wien Nord and Floridsdorf and passes through Wien Mitte. A one-way ticket is valid for one hour and includes transfer to connecting city transport.

Taxi A standard taxi to/from central Vienna costs roughly €35.

TRANSPORT TIMES BETWEEN KEY DESTINATIONS

	Stephansplatz	Schloss Schönbrunn	Riesenrad	Naschmarkt	Museums Quartier
Stephansplatz	n/a	U-Bahn 15min	U-Bahn 5min	walk 20min	U-Bahn 5min
Schloss Schönbrunn	U-Bahn 15min	n/a	U-Bahn 17min	U-Bahn 7min	U-Bahn 17min
Riesenrad	U-Bahn 5min	U-Bahn 17min	n/a	U-Bahn 5min	U-Bahn 10min
Naschmarkt	walk 20min	U-Bahn 7min	U-Bahn 5min	n/a	walk 15min
Museums Quartier	U-Bahn 5min	U-Bahn 17min	U-Bahn 10min	walk 15min	n/a

Vienna has multiple train stations. At the time of writing, a massive construction project was in progress at Vienna's Südbahnhof. An eastern section of the Südbahnhof has been set up as a temporary station called the **Südbahnhof Ostbahn**, which serves some regional trains to/from the east, including Bratislava. All other long-distance trains are being re-routed among the rest of Vienna's train stations, which include **Franz-Josefs-Bahnhof** (which handles trains to/from the Danube Valley), **Meidling**, **Wien Mitte**, **Wien Nord** and **Westbahnhof**.

Once construction at the Südbahnhof is completed, the complex will reopen as the main rail hub and will be called the **Hauptbahnhof Wien** (Vienna Central Station). As the main station, it will receive most international trains. It is slated to be operational in late 2012 or early 2013.

VISAS

Visas are not required for stays of up to 90 days in Austria for citizens of the EU, the EEA (European Economic Area) and Switzerland, much of Eastern Europe, Israel, USA, Canada, the majority of Central and South American nations, Japan, Korea, Malaysia, Singapore, Australia or New Zealand. All other nationalities require a visa. The Ministry of Foreign Affairs' website, www.bmaa.gv.at, has a list of Austrian embassies where you can apply.

If you wish to stay longer, you can leave the country and re-enter. EU nationals can stay indefinitely, but are required by law to register with the *Magistratisches Bezirksamt* (local magistrate's office) if the stay exceeds 60 days.

Austria is part of the Schengen Agreement, which includes all EU states (minus Britain and Ireland) and Switzerland. In practical terms, this means a visa issued by one Schengen country is good for all the other member countries and a passport is not required to move from one to the other.

GETTING AROUND

Vienna has an efficient, unified public transport network. Flat-fare tickets are valid for trains, trams, buses, the underground (U-Bahn) and the S-Bahn regional trains. Services are frequent and you rarely have to wait more than 10 minutes. Sunday through to Thursday, public transport starts at around 5am or 6am; buses (with the exception of night buses) and trams finish between 11pm and midnight and S-Bahn and U-Bahn services between 12.30am and 1am. On Friday and Saturday nights, the U-Bahn runs through to the following morning on a reduced schedule. Free maps and information pamphlets are available from **Wiener Linien** (☎ 7909-100; www.wienerlinien.at, in German).

TICKETS

Tickets and passes can be purchased at U-Bahn stations and in *Tabakladen* (tobacconists). Once bought, tickets need to be validated before starting your journey (except for weekly and monthly tickets); look for small blue boxes at the entrance to U-Bahn stations and on buses and trams. Ticket inspection is infrequent, but if you're caught without a ticket you'll be fined €62, no exceptions.

Single-Ride Tickets

The *Einzelfahrschein* (single ticket; €1.80) is good for one journey, with line changes. It costs €2.20 if purchased on trams and buses (correct change required). The *Streifenkarte* (strip ticket; €7.20) gives you four single tickets on one strip.

Travel Passes

The *24/48/72 Stunden Wien-Karte* (€5.70/10/13.60) offers 24, 48 or 72 hours unlimited travel from

---

CLIMATE CHANGE & TRAVEL

Every form of transport that relies on carbon-based fuel generates CO2, the main cause of human-induced climate change. Modern travel is dependent on aeroplanes, which might use less fuel per kilometre per person than most cars but travel much greater distances. The altitude at which aircraft emit gases (including CO2) and particles also contributes to their climate change impact. Many websites offer 'carbon calculators' that allow people to estimate the carbon emissions generated by their journey and, for those who wish to do so, to offset the impact of the greenhouse gases emitted with contributions to portfolios of climate-friendly initiatives throughout the world. Lonely Planet offsets the carbon footprint of all staff and author travel.

time of validation. The *8-Tage-Karte* (eight-day ticket; €28.80) is valid for eight days, but these do not have to be consecutive days; punch the card as and when you need it. The *Wochenkarte* (weekly ticket; €14) is valid Monday through to Sunday only, and the *Monatskarte* (monthly ticket; €49.50) is valid from the 1st to the last day of the month. Also see *Die Wien-Karte*, right.

U-BAHN

The U-Bahn (subway) is a quick and efficient way of getting around the city. There are five lines, U1 to U4 and U6 (there is no U5). Platforms have timetable information and signs showing the exits and nearby facilities.

TRAMS

There's something romantic about travelling by tram, even though they're slower than the U-Bahn. Vienna's tram network is extensive and it's the perfect way to view the city on the cheap. Trams are either numbered or lettered (eg 1, 44, D) and services cover the city centre and some suburbs.

BUS

Buses go everywhere, including inside the Innere Stadt, and are numbered with either three digits or a number followed by an 'A' or 'B'. Very logically, buses connect-

ing with a tram service often have the same number, eg bus 38A connects with tram 38, bus 72A with tram 72.

S-BAHN

S-Bahn trains (designated by a number preceded by an 'S') service the suburbs and satellite towns. If you're travelling outside of Vienna, and outside of the ticket zone, you'll probably have to purchase an extension; check on maps posted in train stations.

CYCLING

Cycling is an excellent way to get around and explore the city – over 800km of cycle tracks criss-cross the capital. Popular cycling areas include the 7km path around the Ringstrasse, the Donauinsel (Danube Island), the Prater and along the Danube Canal (Donaukanal). There are a number of options for keen cyclists.

Vienna has a bike scheme called **Vienna City Bike** (☎ 0810-50 05 00; www.citybikewien.at, in German; 1st hr free, 2nd hr €1, 3rd hr €2, 4th hr & above €4). Currently, over 60 bike stands, provided by the City of Vienna, are scattered throughout the city. A credit card is required to rent bikes – just swipe your card in the machine and follow the instructions (in a number of languages). Keep in mind that these bikes are mainly for use as an alternative to public transport (unless you bring your own bike chain, they can only be locked up at a bike station). A lost bike will set you back €600.

Alternatively, hire a bike at a regular bike shop. The following offer significant information about where to cycle, including maps and local tips.

Copa Cagrana Rad und Skaterverleih (Map p106, G3; ☎ 263 52 42; www .fahrradverleih.at, in German; 22, Am Kaisermühlendamm 1; 1hr/½-/full-day rental from €5/15/25; ⏰ 9am-6pm Mar & Oct, to 8pm Apr & Sep, to 9pm May-Aug; Ⓤ U1 Kaisermühlen). All manner of bikes are on offer here – city, mountain, trekking, tandem, kids' and more. Also rents roller blades (from €6 per hour).

Pedal Power (Map p106, D5; ☎ 729 72 34; www.pedalpower.at; 02, Ausstellungsstrasse 3; 1hr/½-/full-day rental €5/24/32; ⏰ 8am-7pm Apr-Oct; Ⓤ U1, U2 Praterstern). Pick up city or mountain bikes at the office or, for an extra €4, arrange for them to be dropped off and picked up at your hotel.

TAXI

Taxis in Vienna are reliable and relatively cheap by Western European standards. City journeys are metered; flag fall costs roughly €2.60 from 6am to 11pm Monday to Saturday and €2.70 any other time, plus a small per km fee. A small tip is expected; add about 10% onto the fare. Taxis are easily found at train stations and taxi stands all over the city, or just flag them down in the street. To order

one call ☎ 31 300, 60 160 or 40 100. Few accept credit cards.

PRACTICALITIES
BUSINESS HOURS

Banks open from 8am or 9am to 3pm Monday to Friday, with extended hours, to 5.30pm, on Thursday. Many smaller branches close from 12.30pm to 1.30pm.

Restaurants are open from 11am to 11pm or midnight, while cafes operate 7am to midnight. Post offices are generally open 8am to noon and 2pm to 6pm Monday to Friday, and some are also open 8am to noon Saturday. Shops are usually open 9am to 6pm Monday to Friday and until 5pm Saturday; some have extended hours on Thursday or Friday, to 9pm.

DISCOUNTS

The *Die Wien-Karte* (Vienna Card; €18.50) allows three days unlimited travel on the public transport system (including night buses) and provides discounts at selected museums, cafes, *Heurigen* (wine taverns), restaurants and shops across the city, and on guided tours and the CAT (see the boxed text, p157). The discount usually amounts to 5% to 10% off the normal price, or a free gift. The card can be purchased at Tourist-Info Wien (p162) and many top hotel concierge desks.

INFORMATION

As well as the excellent official websites, there are a few other sites that offer good insights and information on travelling to Vienna.

Falter (www.falter.at, in German) Vienna's listings newspaper – a wealth of information for what's on.

MuseumsQuartier (www.mqw.at) All about the MQ and its venues. By clicking on 'Links' (at the bottom) you reach a great list of hotlinks to other cultural institutions.

Tourist-Info Wien (www.wien.info) The main official Vienna city tourist information website. As well as having the more usual offerings, it has sections such as www.vienna hype.at, which has a more happening angle.

Vienna Metblogs (http://vienna.metblogs. com) This multilingual blog site ranges from the banal to the inspiring and insightful.

Vienna Webservice (www.wien.gv.at) The official Vienna City Council website, with everything from the current weather to interactive maps for address searches and information on sights, as well as services for Viennese residents.

Virtual Vienna Net (www.virtualvienna.net) Informative non-official website with a forum and some good articles, such as on the Jewish Vienna pages.

Wieninternational (www.wieninternational. at) Weekly bilingual (German and English) on-line magazine with short and feature articles all aspects of culture, economy and society, with a focus on European integration.

NET

wishing to stay in ail while on holiday

will have no problems in Vienna. Many of the main streets leading away from the city centre outside the Gürtel are lined with cheap, albeit slightly grungy, call centres doubling as internet cafes. Additionally, a large number of coffee houses, cafes and many bars have free or low-cost internet. Look for the wi-fi sign; they're called WLAN hot spots.

Most hotels have wi-fi or internet, but as yet it's not possible to organise an ISP in Austria for a short period (minimum contracts run for 12 months). For a relatively up-to-date list of venues offering free wi-fi, see www.freewave. at/en/hotspots; you can use the handy drop-down menu to search by district (1010 for the first, 1110 for the 10th, etc).

LANGUAGE

BASICS

Hello.	*Hallo./Guten Tag.*
Goodbye.	*Auf Wiedersehen.*
Please.	*Bitte.*
Thank you.	*Danke.*
Yes./No.	*Ja./Nein.*
Do you speak English?	*Sprechen Sie Englisch?*
How much is it?	*Wie viel kostet es?*

EMERGENCIES

I'm sick.	*Ich bin krank.*
Help!	*Hilfe!*

Call the	Rufen Sie
police!	die Polizei!
Call an	Rufen Sie einen
ambulance!	Krankenwagen!

MONEY

Austria's currency is the euro, which is divided into 100 cents. There are coins for one, two, five, 10, 20 and 50 cents, and €1 and €2. Notes come in denominations of €5, €10, €20, €50, €100, €200 and €500.

See the Quick Reference (inside front cover) for exchange rates at the time of press. For the latest rates, check out www.xe.com.

On average, staying at a two- to four-star hotel, eating out twice a day, taking in a show and a couple of museums and downing a few cups of coffee will set you back around €170 to €250 per day. Anyone staying in dorms in hostels and eating at budget restaurants can expect to survive for about €45 to €50 per day.

ORGANISED TOURS

DDSG Blue Danube (Map p36, G2; ☎ 588 80; www.ddsg-blue-danube.at; 01, Schwedenbrücke; adult/under 10yr/concession from €15/free/7.50; ☼ tours 11am & 3pm Apr-Oct; ⊚ U1, U4 Schwedenplatz ⍾ 1, 2) Boats cover a variety of tour routes; some of the most popular include circumnavigating Leopoldstadt and Brigittenau districts using the Danube Canal and the Danube as their thoroughfare.

Fiaker (20min/40min/1hr tours €40/65/95) More of a tourist novelty than anything else, a *Fiaker* is a traditional-style open carriage drawn by a pair of horses. Lines of horses, carriages and bowler-hatted drivers can be found at Stephansplatz, Albertinaplatz and Heldenplatz at the Hofburg.

Ring Tram (☎ 790 91 00; www.wiener linien.at; adult/child €6/4; ☼ 10am-6pm Sep-Jun, to 7pm Jul & Aug; ⊚ U1, U4 Schwedenplatz ⍾ 1, 2) Runs the length of the Ringstrasse and is essentially a hop-on, hop-off service with video screens and guided commentary along the way.

Verliebt in Wien (☎ 889 28 06; www.ver liebtinwien.at; adult/child €12/6; ☼ Jun-Oct; ⊚ U1, U2, U4 Karlsplatz ⍾ D, 1, 2 ⍾ 59A, 62) Margarete Kirschner offers themed walks covering topics such as Medieval Vienna, art nouveau, and Hundertwasser and modern architecture. Tours take around 1½ to two hours.

Vienna Walks' Third Man Tour (☎ 774 89 01; www.viennawalks.com; tickets €17; ☼ English tours 4pm Mon & Fri) Tours depart from the U4 Stadtpark station (Johannesgasse exit), and cover all the main locations used in the film, including a glimpse of the underground sewers, home to 2.5 million rats.

TELEPHONE

Austria uses the GSM 900/1800 cellular system, compatible with phones from the rest of Europe, Australia and most of Asia, and dual-band GSM 1900/900 phones from North America.

Telekom Austria (☎ 0800 100 100; www.telekom.at, in German) is Austria's main telecommunications provider and maintains a variety of public telephones throughout Vienna. These take either coins or phonecards and a minimum of €0.20 is required to make a local call. Many post offices have phone booths where both international and national calls can be made; rates are cheaper from 6pm to 8am Monday to Friday, and on weekends.

COUNTRY & CITY CODES
Country code (☎ 43)
Vienna city code (☎ 01)

USEFUL PHONE NUMBERS
Emergency (police, fire, ambulance) (☎ 112)
International access code (☎ 00)
Local directory inquiries (☎ 11 88 77)
Taxi (☎ 31 300, 40 100)

TIPPING
Tipping is part of everyday life in Vienna. In service establishments, it's customary to round up smaller bills (to the nearest 50 cents or euro) when buying coffee or beer, and to add 10% to the bill for full meals. Taxi drivers will also expect around 10% extra. Tips are handed over at the time of payment: add the bill and tip together and pass it over in one lump sum.

TOURIST INFORMATION
Vienna's main tourist office, **Tourist Info Wien** (Map p36, D5; ☎ 211 14; www. wien.info; 01, Albertinaplatz; ⏱ 9am-7pm) contains a ticket agency, hotel booking service, free maps and every brochure under the sun. There's also an **Airport Information Office** (⏱ 6am-11pm) located in the arrivals hall. The **City Hall Info Office** (Rathaus Information Office; Map p36, A3; ☎ 525 50; www.wien.gv.at; 01, Rathaus; ⏱ 8am-6pm Mon-Fri) provides information on social, cultural and practical matters.

TRAVELLERS WITH DISABILITIES
Vienna is fairly well geared to people with disabilities *(Behinderte)*, but not exceptionally so. Ramps are common but by no means ubiquitous; most U-Bahn stations have wheelchair lifts, but trams and buses don't (though buses can lower themselves for easier access and the newer trams have doors at ground level); many, but once again not all, traffic lights 'bleep' to indicate when pedestrians can safely cross the road.

NOTES

>INDEX

See also separate subindexes for Drink (p172), Eat (p173), Play (p173), See (p174) and Shop (p175).

000 map pages

000 map pages

DRINK

Bars
Bricks Lazy Dancebar 112
Café Leopold 66
Chelsea 79
Das Möbel 66-7
Elektro Gönner 67
Europa 67
Filmbar im Kesselhaus 129
Futuregarden Bar & Art Club 67
Joanelli 67-8
Kunsthallencafé 93
Mon Ami 68
Orange One 94
Palmenhaus 52-3
Phil 68
Rhiz 80-1
Rote Bar 69-70
Schikaneder 94
Tachles 112
Tanzcafé Jenseits 69
Top Kino Bar 69
Wirr 69

Cafes
Café Leopold 66
Café Sperl 66
Das Möbel 66-7
Europa 67
Kunsthallencafé 93
Palmenhaus 52-3
Phil 68
Tachles 112

Clubs
Bricks Lazy Dancebar 112
Chelsea 79
Futuregarden Bar & Art Club 67
Rhiz 80-1
Tanzcafé Jenseits 69

Cocktail Bars
Ebert's Cocktail Bar 67
Halbestadt 78, 79-80
Kruger's American Bar 52, 78
Loos American Bar 52, 89
Shiraz 81

Coffee Houses
Aida 50
Café Alt Wien 50
Café Domayer 121
Café Drechsler 65
Café Gloriette 122
Café Hummel 79
Café Prückel 50-2
Café Rüdigerhof 93
Café Sacher 51, 52

Gay Bars
Café Berg 79
Frauencafé 79
Mango Bar 68

Heurigen
Edlmoser 122
Hirt 80
Mayer am Pfarrplatz 80
Reinprecht 80
Zahel 122

Hookah Bars
Shiraz 81

Microbreweries
Salm Bräu 103
Siebensternbräu 68-9

Pubs & Beer Gardens
Brandauer's Schlossbräu 120
Piano 130

Stadtheurigen
Weinstube Josefstadt 81-2
Zwölf Apostelkeller 53

🛍 SHOP

INDEX